THE COMMUNITY
COLLEGE GUIDE

Debra Gonsher, Ph.D.,
and Joshua Halberstam, Ph.D.

THE COMMUNITY COLLEGE GUIDE

The Essential Reference from Application to Graduation

BENBELLA BOOKS, INC.
Dallas, Texas

Copyright © 2009 by Debra Gonsher Vinik, Ph.D., and Joshua Halberstam, Ph.D.

BENBELLA

BenBella Books, Inc.
6440 N. Central Expressway, Suite 503
Dallas, TX 75206
www.benbellabooks.com
Send feedback to feedback@benbellabooks.com

Printed in the United States of America
10 9 8 7 6 5 4 3 2 1

Library of Congress Cataloging-in-Publication Data is available for this title.
ISBN 978-1933771-73-1

Proofreading by Emily Chauviere and Gregory Teague
Cover design by Melody Cadungog
Text design and composition by John Reinhardt Book Design
Printed by Bang Printing

Distributed by Perseus Distribution
perseusdistribution.com

To place orders through Perseus Distribution:
Tel: 800-343-4499
Fax: 800-351-5073
E-mail: orderentry@perseusbooks.com

Significant discounts for bulk sales are available.
Please contact Glenn Yeffeth at glenn@benbellabooks.com or (214) 750-3628.

Contents

Contents

Part Two: GET AHEAD

Preface

EVERYONE SEEMS TO BE TALKING about community college these days. It's no wonder: community college has long been one of the best deals in town, but with the economy as difficult as it is now, the appeal of community college is stronger than ever. And those who are looking at community college for the first time are surprised to discover that these schools are providing some of the most innovative programs around, from tribal art to zoology.

We, of course, have known about this unheralded treasure for years. We've been working in community college as teachers, mentors, and chairpersons, witnessing first-hand the success of our students. And to tell the truth, we've also been frustrated by the bad rap community college has received for so long. Too many haven't recognized these schools as serious institutions of learning, and even more have simply ignored community college altogether.

That neglect is perhaps most visibly represented by the absence of books aimed at the community college student. Step into any bookstore and visit the college section and you'll see rows of books with flashy titles all directed at the four-year-college student—everything from how to choose a college to books advising you on how to deal with your obnoxious roommate once you get there. But for community college students? Just about nothing.

This book helps fill this gaping void.

We had a few essential goals in writing this book. One, we wanted to be comprehensive. Community college students need hard facts that deal with real world challenges, including: how to apply, how to register, the degree options they can choose from, and how to pay for—or get grants to pay for—their education. Indeed, you'll find here an almost encyclopedic review of what you need to know to successfully navigate the maze of community college.

Second, we wanted to provide students with practical strategies on how to succeed in school: dealing with their professors, study tips, note-taking, test-taking skills, writing term papers, and the other things one needs to understand to be a first-rate student.

Third, we wanted to review what community college students need to know as they prepare to move on with the next phase of their lives. And so you'll also find here essential information on how to transfer to a four-year college, as well as how to prepare and enter the job market. You'll get advice on how to network, write a dynamite resume, and excel at your interview.

In each chapter, you'll find information that deals with the specific issues important to you. You'll notice intriguing asides we've called **Who Would've Thought**? that provide tidbits about community colleges, courses of study, program origins, and other surprising factoids. We've also included asides called **Digging Deeper** that invite you to investigate further any topics that have stimulated your interest. And we've contributed some insights from our own experiences called **From the Authors' Files**.

One of the most useful sections of this book is the appendix. We've put together a list of Web sites to help you explore the subjects we've covered. And in case you're too tired to type, you can access this list and associated links on our Web site, http://www.thecommunitycollegeguide.com—or for those of you who have a plane to catch, http://www.cc-guide.com. If you have suggestions for additional sites for the next time around (or other comments or suggestions about the book), please get in touch with us at profs@cc-guide.com.

When you've had a chance to skip around this book, you'll note just how much information we've compiled here—no easy task. So we want to take a moment to thank some of the people who made this possible. Dr. Isabel Mirsky contributed her awesome knowledge about the ins and outs of community college and offered it all with her usual generosity of spirit. Our agent, Carol Mann, understood this was an important book and wouldn't give up until she found a publisher. And she did so by bringing it to Glenn Yeffeth at BenBella, who enrolled his terrific staff to tend to the book, including our editor Leah Wilson and her wonderful team. And last but most, we'd like to thank the two people who so enrich our lives every morning and every night and give us the space and encouragement to get projects like this done, our dear spouses, David (Debra's husband) and Yoko (Joshua's wife). We love you more than all the words in this book.

This guide is for those who are contemplating attending community college, those who have just enrolled, and those who are already attending. Wherever you are in your education timeline, you'll find here the information and advice you need to know to flourish in community college. Here are our good wishes for an outstanding college career and beyond.

Debra Gonsher
Joshua Halberstam
August 4, 2009

GET READY

PART ONE

*Choosing an accredited community college
is one of the smartest decisions
you will make in your academic career.*

The Why of Community College...and the Who, What, and Where

MORE THAN 11 MILLION PEOPLE attend community college in the United States, nearly half the nation's college student population. Are you considering joining them? If you've already enrolled, are you still wondering if you made the right decision? For many of these millions of students, perhaps even most, community college is not only a good choice, but the best choice. It might be your best choice as well.

THE BENEFITS OF COMMUNITY COLLEGE

Here are some of the advantages you should consider when deciding whether choosing community college makes sense for you.

Affordability

Community college isn't free, but compared to most four-year colleges, it's a true bargain. According to the American Association of Community Colleges, in the 2008–2009 year, the average annual tuition for a community college was $2,402. Compare this with $6,585, which is the average tuition at a public four-year college; you gain a difference of more than $4,000 each year. Add room and board, and the difference in cost is even greater.[1] The cost for private colleges is much, much higher—at some schools, tuition and board for college is now more than $50,000 a year!

WHO WOULD'VE THOUGHT?

The U.S. Department of Education, too, recommends enrolling in a community college as a way to save money. See its "Keeping the Cost of College Down" Web page at http://www.ed.gov/students/prep/college/thinkcollege/early/parents/edlite-cost-down.html#four.

Your community college expenses can be even less if you are awarded scholarships or grants (we review how to access these resources in Chapter 3, "Money Matters"). But with or without financial aid, community college is a savvy financial alternative.

Location

Many students choose community college because of its geographical convenience. If you have children or a job in the area, it's clearly an advantage to be able to sit in your classes ten minutes after the babysitter arrives or fifteen minutes after you finish eight hours of work.

WHO WOULD'VE THOUGHT?

The term "community college" derives from the fact that the schools draw students primarily from the local community and are often supported by the local community through property taxes. Before the 1980s, community colleges were commonly referred to as junior colleges, a term still used at some institutions. In New Jersey, Texas, and Illinois they are sometimes called county colleges.

Geography counts, but it shouldn't be the only factor in your decision. What matters even more is the availability of the program you want to study. For example, if you want to eventually work as a paralegal, and your nearby community college doesn't provide this program, it might make sense to travel farther out of your comfort zone to obtain the education and job you desire.

Flexibility

Do you work? Have family obligations? These commitments can make managing a regular college timetable difficult, if not impossible. At four-year schools, classes are mostly limited to daytime hours with night classes few and far between. At a community college, on the other hand, you'll find multiple sections of the same course, some given early in the morning and some late at night, and classes available seven days a week. You can, therefore, shape a schedule that suits your busy life and take your classes before work, during the day, in the evening, over the weekend, or online.

DIGGING DEEPER

Check out your prospective school for its schedule of class times. Most community colleges have classes that begin at 8:00 A.M. but some start as early as 7:00 A.M. In addition, some schools offer full weekend programs with classes Friday night and all day Saturday and Sunday.

Flexibility doesn't only refer to taking classes when you want them, but also to the number of classes you wish to take during a semester. Unlike most four-year colleges, which expect their students to attend full time, community college makes being a part-time student an option for those who choose this route. In fact, two-thirds of community college students attend part time.[2]

A Wide Choice of Programs

Community colleges offer a range of study options. You can concentrate on a broad liberal arts education or focus on a particular profession. You can pursue an associate's degree and then continue your education at a four-year college, or prepare for immediate employment in a new career. You can also acquire a certificate that will enhance your skills in your present occupation. Of the wide field of programs that community colleges often offer, you're likely to find one that suits your talents and career goals.

WHO WOULD'VE THOUGHT?

The average expected lifetime earnings for a graduate with an associate's degree is $1.6 million—about a half million more than a high school graduate earns.[3]

For some career programs, community college is the number one place to study. For example, 80 percent of American firefighters, law enforcement officers, and emergency medical technicians are trained at community colleges. So, depending on your career goals, community college may not only be a good choice but the clear choice.

We should note, too, the growing popularity of community colleges for international students. These students are eager to benefit from community colleges' preparatory programs, remedial classes, and English courses that ready them for their careers or transition to a four-year college. International students also realize that community college makes good financial sense!

Dedicated Faculty

Unlike many of the faculty at four-year colleges, community college professors focus on teaching. Their attention is not focused primarily on research and scholarly writing but on their students. And unlike four-year schools, no classes in community college are taught by graduate teaching assistants.

Faculty at community colleges have attained at least a master's degree or its equivalent, and many have doctorates in their fields. In addition, faculty in programs geared toward careers upon graduation, such as the Associate in Applied Science (AAS) degree (see "Choosing Your Educational Program" in Chapter 2), often have direct connections to their respective industries. These ties can be of enormous help in furthering your career goals.

Smaller Class Size Means Greater Student–Teacher Interaction

It's not uncommon in four-year colleges to have large lecture classes with hundreds of students—in stark contrast to community college classes, which rarely have more than forty students and usually many fewer. No wonder community college students consistently report classroom experiences of greater interaction, discussion, and one-on-one opportunities than do students in universities.

WHO WOULD'VE THOUGHT?

In a recent survey students at community college listed as their greatest satisfaction the quality of instruction in their classes.[4]

Interesting Classmates

One of community college's richest assets is the diversity of its students. Of course you can meet interesting classmates at a four-year school as well, but community college students are likely to be much more varied: old and young, men and women, some with degrees, some not. The broad spectrum of students helps make community college a special learning experience.

Try this short quiz to see how well you know your classmates.

WHO ATTENDS COMMUNITY COLLEGE?

1. What percentage of community college students is twenty-two years or older?
   - ___ A. 20%
   - ___ B. 36%
   - ___ C. 44%
   - ___ D. 58%

2. What percentage of community college students is female?
   - ___ A. 35%
   - ___ B. 50%
   - ___ C. 59%
   - ___ D. 70%

3. What percentage of community college students has at least one parent who completed a bachelor's degree or higher?
   - ___ A. 5%
   - ___ B. 20%
   - ___ C. 39%
   - ___ D. 51%

4. What percentage of nurses in the United States is educated at community colleges?
   - ___ A. 15%
   - ___ B. 30%
   - ___ C. 50%
   - ___ D. 75%

5. How many international students are currently enrolled in an American community college?
   - ___ A. 10,000
   - ___ B. 25,000
   - ___ C. 50,000
   - ___ D. 100,000

Answers: 1. D, 2. C, 3. C, 4. C, 5. D

Successful Transfer To Four-Year Schools

This will come as a surprise to many, but community college students have a better chance of getting into four-year colleges than students transferring from other four-year schools. As we'll see in our discussion of transferring in Chapter 15, many community colleges have articulation agreements (programs that guarantee acceptance of credits) with four-year colleges that ease the transfer from one school to the next. Even less well known is that community college students who do transfer perform as well as students who began in four-year schools.[5] Clearly, the education at two-year schools provides the preparation one needs to move on in higher education. No wonder, then, that four-year colleges often give priority to students transferring from community colleges, citing their demonstrated preparedness for senior college-level work.

A Time to Adjust

For many younger college students, the move from home to the dormitory environment of college is stressful and overwhelming. Many of these students flounder during this transitional phase, wasting their time and money. A two-year college, on the other hand, may allow you to continue to live at home, not only saving you money but also providing a transitional period in which to ease yourself into independence. You'll have time to get comfortable being a college student and an opportunity to explore career options before committing yourself to a single path.

A Second Chance

Were you an underachiever in high school? Did you never before consider higher education? Do you think you're not ready for a four-year college? Community college is your home for second chances. Here you can start afresh and attain a high grade point average that will open the doors of the best four-year schools. If you're unprepared for college in some areas, remedial classes will help you become more than prepared. Supply the commitment, and in community college you'll find the opportunity to excel.

FROM THE AUTHORS' FILES

Arguably, the best part of community college for faculty and students alike is graduation day. Walking down the quadrangle path, "Pomp and Circumstance" blaring, I marvel at the students who managed to make it through to this commencement, this "beginning." Susan, an LPN who returned to school to study radiologic technology; Miguel, who had gotten his GED in the military; Lea, whose parents had lost money in the stock market downturn; and the valedictorian, Venezuelan-born Luis, a media technology major who had come to the United States as a young man, and in his thirties decided he wanted to become a producer of music videos. This episode may be a funny thing to bring up at the beginning of this book—the start of your journey—but then again, it is always good to keep your eye on the final destination. *DG*

ACCREDITATION MATTERS

You've decided to attend community college, and your next question is which one? As the appeal of two-year colleges grows, students are now presented with more choices than ever before. In addition to considering the factors listed previously—finances, location, program of study, and flexibility of program—you also need to confirm that the college you're considering is accredited.

Accreditation is certification that an institution meets set standards of quality. If a college is not accredited, you may want to think twice about enrolling there. Here's why:

- You cannot qualify for any government-sponsored financial aid if you attend a nonaccredited college.
- The majority of employers who offer tuition assistance will only reimburse your tuition costs from an institution that has accreditation.
- Credits from a nonaccredited college will generally not transfer to an accredited college.
- Potential employers will look less favorably at a degree from a nonaccredited school.

Although the U.S. Department of Education does not itself provide accreditation, as that is usually done by one of six regional agencies such as the Middle States Association of Colleges and Schools, it does provide a search engine that shows whether your school is accredited: http://www.ope.ed.gov/accreditation/Search.aspx. If you are uncertain whether your college is accredited, take the time to make sure it is.

AND REMEMBER...

Community colleges are student-oriented institutions with dedicated faculties that provide their students with a wonderful academic experience and a path to future educational and career advancement. For so many, enrolling at a community college is a smart choice. The U.S. government knows it, financial institutions know it, and students from around the world know it, as do some of the best in the world's entertainment, business, and sciences fields. Community college can be a life-changing experience. The resources are waiting. You only need to bring the best of yourself.

COMMUNITY COLLEGE ALUMNI

You're Joining an Outstanding Group

Entertainment

Jim Belushi, television actor/comedian; *According to Jim*

Billy Crystal, comedian/actor; *City Slickers*, *Analyze This*

Clint Eastwood, actor/director; *Million Dollar Baby*, *Flags of Our Fathers*, *Changeling*

Tom Hanks, actor; *Cast Away*, *Forrest Gump*, *The Da Vinci Code*, *Angels and Demons*

Diane Keaton, actress; *Father of the Bride*, *From Zero to Sixty*

Queen Latifah, singer/actress; *Beauty Shop*, *The Secret Life of Bees*

George Lucas, producer/director; the Star Wars series

John Mellencamp, singer/songwriter; "Hurts So Good," "Jack and Diane"

Sylvester Stallone, actor; *Rambo*, *Rocky*

John Walsh, host; *America's Most Wanted*

Robin Williams, comedian/actor; *Mrs. Doubtfire*, *Good Will Hunting*, *August Rush*, *The Krazees*

Writers

Gwendolyn Brooks, Pulitzer Prize-winning poet; "Do Not Be Afraid
of No," "The Bean Eaters"
Rita Mae Brown, author; *Rubyfruit Jungle*
Amy Tan, author; *The Joy Luck Club*, *The Bonesetter's Daughter*

Sports

Laila Ali, boxer; *Dancing with the Stars*
Pete Rozelle, former commissioner of the NFL
Nolan Ryan, Hall of Fame pitcher
Venus Williams, Grand Slam tennis champion

Business Leaders

Walt Disney, founder of the Disney empire
Calvin Klein, fashion designer
H. Ross Perot, former presidential candidate/founder of Electronic
Data Systems (EDS)
Melvin Salveson, creator of MasterCard
James Sinegal, CEO of Costco

Government

Arthur Goldberg, former Supreme Court Justice
Kweisi Mfume, former president of the NAACP
Arnold Schwarzenegger, former actor/current governor of California

Science and Technology

Eileen Collins, astronaut
Fred Haise, astronaut
Francis Scobee, astronaut
Craig Venter, mapped the genome

The community college application process calls for careful attention to the entry requirements and procedures: what you need to get in, what you have to do to get in, and what you will study when you do get in.

The Application Process in Twenty Documents or Less

YOU'VE DECIDED TO ATTEND A COMMUNITY COLLEGE. Great idea. Your school has the program you want to study, it's conveniently located, and it's cost effective. Now you're wondering: What do I have to do to get in and begin taking classes?

Applying to a community college is a process with important steps, each demanding careful attention. There will be forms to fill out, deadlines to meet, and choices to make. But considering what you receive in return, dealing efficiently with all these preliminaries is well worth the effort. This chapter will help you through the process.

REQUIREMENTS FOR ACCEPTANCE

You may have heard that anyone can get in to a community college, that you don't need to submit any information, and that you can just roll out of bed or jump off your skateboard and start attending school. Well, it's not that simple. There are conditions that must be satisfied and documents that must be filed.

Academic Requirements

The first set of documents you will have to deal with relates to your academic background.

Open Admissions

Community colleges operate under a policy of "open admissions." This means anyone with a high school diploma or GED equivalency has an opportunity to further his or her education. (GED is an acronym for General Educational Development. It's a certificate awarded to those who successfully pass a series of tests measuring educational level in five basic areas.) Even if you did poorly in high school, community college provides a chance to begin anew. In fact, even if you haven't graduated high school or received a GED but are eighteen or older, you can be admitted to a community college in California.[1] And if your state does require a high school degree or GED, and you have neither, your community college might provide noncredit classes to help you prepare for the GED exam.

But note that admission to a community college does not guarantee admission to a selective admissions program. Most of these selective admissions programs are in health care or technology fields. These are competitive programs whose admission requirements are often more demanding than those required for admission to the college.

 DIGGING DEEPER

The SAT Reasoning Test and ACT (American College Testing assessment) are national standardized tests generally required for admission to four-year colleges. Some community colleges ask that you take the SAT or ACT exam as well, but rarely do they require this for admittance. Instead, they use the tests to help place students in appropriate classes or to determine if they are eligible for an honors program.

One benefit of this open admissions policy is that your classmates will represent a wide range of backgrounds: students who excelled in high school, students who barely passed, and some who have obtained a high school degree later in their lives. You'll have classmates who have been successful in one career (administrative assistant, for example), but now want to embark on a new one (nuclear medical technician) and others who are looking to improve their skills in their present professions. Many of your fellow students are on their way to a four-year college, while others expect to enter their new fields immediately upon graduation.

But open admissions does not mean that once admitted you can enroll for any course you like; eligibility for many classes requires that you've met certain academic standards. In all likelihood, even if you have a high school diploma or a GED, or you're returning to school after many years, you'll need to take placement tests in English and math to demonstrate proficiency in basic college-level skills.

Transferring from Another College

If you are transferring from another two- or four-year college, you'll have to provide a transcript of the work you've done. (You may also be asked to supply your scores on previous placement tests.) Your main concern is transferring the credits you've already earned. Don't assume that the class you took in your previous college has an equivalent in your new college and that you'll automatically get credit for it. On the other hand, don't assume that the classes are so different that you won't get credit for the course. Contact the admissions office of the community college to which you're transferring to find out what documentation you need to supply. It'll be easier for your new college and corresponding departments to decide whether to grant credit if you show them a copy of the description and syllabus from each of the courses you've taken elsewhere. In fact, provide everything about your past classes—weekly breakdowns of assignments, any papers or tests—that you think might bolster your case for receiving credit.

International Students

Applicants who attended school outside the United States should provide paperwork that confirms their schooling. If these documents are not in English, you'll need to have them translated and certified. If you've attended a college outside the United States, you may want to submit your transcript to one of the many services that evaluate academic credentials, such as North American Educational Group (http://www.naeg.org) or the Academic Credentials Evaluation Institute (http://www.aceil.com). Make sure to get a comprehensive evaluation that lists all of your courses, the credits awarded, and your grades. Most international students will also need to provide a student visa.[2]

Community colleges welcome international students, and most, if not all, have an office that deals with the specific concerns of this student population. If you're an international student, get in touch with this office as soon as possible. Here you'll learn what conditions you must meet to study in the United States and receive visa/status advisement, forms with which to apply for a change in status and reinstatement, and information on travel issues and Social Security. You'll also learn about your eligibility to work in the United States.

Your contact with your school's office for international students shouldn't end with your application to attend. These offices help international students acclimate to the United States by providing a place to meet and hosting events, parties, and off-campus educational and recreational experiences. The earlier you access this resource and remain in contact with it, the smoother your road to study in the United States and transition to your new environment will be.

What You Won't Need

Here are two things you won't need when applying to community college. One, letters of recommendation. Don't throw away any wonderful letter someone wrote on your behalf—you might attach it to an application for a job or an internship—but it's not required for community college. And, two, you don't need to worry about an interview; that, also, isn't required for admission to a community college. This is good news: you can use for your textbooks the money you were planning to spend for an interview outfit.

WHO WOULD'VE THOUGHT?

A few schools are beginning to require some very specialized academic requirements. Valencia Community College in Orlando, Florida, for example, requires an audition for acceptance to their AA in Dance Performance degree.

Residency Requirements

Students from anywhere are eligible to enroll in community college if they meet the academic and age requirements. But because community colleges are established to serve the residents of their geographic regions, state inhabitants often receive preference with regard to admission and tuition. The college in which you are interested may have additional preferences for those who live in the same city or township as the community college.

Note, however, that a number of states have reciprocity agreements that allow residents of a neighboring state to be considered as a resident of the other. In addition, members of the military are often exempted from residency requirements.

States vary in their definitions of residency and what they regard as proof of residency. FastWeb's College Gold is a helpful site that will direct you to the residency requirements of your state. You can access it at http://www.collegegold.com/applydecide/staterequirements.

If you have any questions about whether you meet residency requirements or what documentation you need to provide to prove your residency, contact the admissions office at your college. Find out, too, when you need to submit the necessary paperwork and how you can appeal the school's decision if you disagree with its determination.

DOCUMENTS THAT CAN ESTABLISH RESIDENCY

- Employer contract or letter verifying the dates of employment
- Copy of your state income tax forms
- Driver's license
- Automobile registration
- Copy of your parent's/guardian's latest personal income tax forms
- Long-term lease, rental, or home purchase agreement
- Voter registration
- Statement from public and/or private agencies attesting to your residency for a specific period of time

---

Immunization Requirements

If you were born after January 1, 1957, and are applying to college for the first time, you must submit proof of immunization. Many states mandate that no community college accept students who do not submit immunization papers as part of their applications. Other community colleges will permit you to register and even attend classes for a thirty-day grace period, after which you'll be barred from classes if you haven't produced evidence of immunization. Acceptable evidence includes immunization cards from childhood, immunization records from high school or other schools you attended, or records from your doctor or clinic.

The timetable for colleges may vary, but in all instances, you will need proof of immunization. If you cannot provide this proof, you will need to be immunized again.

FORMS, DEADLINES, AND FEES

Applying to college entails knowing where to submit your application, filling out the forms in a timely manner, and perhaps forking over a bit of your hard-earned cash.

Where to Apply

Some states allow you to submit one application for any community college in the state; you can, for example, apply to any of the 109 community colleges in California with a single application. But most community colleges have their own application processes with their own admission policies, deadlines, and document requirements. Therefore, you need to contact the college and ask for the appropriate application materials. Don't assume that the application process in one school is the same as in another.

Deadlines

Among your first steps in applying to school is finding out what supporting materials need to be submitted and when they are due. This information is probably on the school's Web site, but don't hesitate to call the college's admissions office if you have any questions about requirements and deadlines.

The time factor is crucial, because knowing when to apply will guide you on how to apply. Applying early has advantages. You'll probably be able to file your application online (good for your busy schedule) and apply to a number of colleges at the same time with a single application fee. But these options have a time limit, so get going on the application as soon as possible. Too many applicants miss deadlines by only a few days; it'd be a shame if this happens to you.

FROM THE AUTHORS' FILES

I hate thinking about all the opportunities I squandered because I didn't want to bother with the application process. All those job possibilities, grant proposals, home mortgages...ah, the list is way too long. You know the saying "Penny wise, dollar stupid"? It works that way with time. When I meet people who don't bother applying to community college because it's such a drag filling out the forms and takes too long, I want to grab them and scream, "Don't be minute smart and lifetime stupid!" Take the time. Do the application. And do it right. You'll be so sorry later if you don't. *JH*

Don't expect to complete your application overnight. For example, it can take weeks—even months—to receive and submit your high school transcript to the college. Your accompanying financial aid request might involve unforeseen bottlenecks as well.

A general rule to remember about the application process is that you should expect everything to take twice as long as you expect. (Come to think of it, that's a good rule for everything we set out to do in our lives.) If you're lucky and your application goes through smoothly and quickly, all the sweeter. But if not, you'll have enough time to deal with any issues that arise and not miss the start of a new term.

Rolling Admissions

Many community colleges offer rolling admissions, which means you can apply any time of the year. You'll need, therefore, to specify which semester you'd like to begin. A semester is a period of study, usually of about fifteen weeks. There are two semesters a year in most colleges, plus the summer session. Some schools are organized with three semesters plus the summer. This is referred to as either a trimester system (because there are three semesters during the "regular" school year) or a quarter system (in reference to the four semesters over the entire year). Make sure to find out the framework in which your college operates and decide on the semester you want to begin.

Application Fees

There's a wide range in application fees to community colleges, from $0 (in some states) to a small charge of $10 or $15, to the more substantial fee of $60 (the City University of New York) and perhaps even more elsewhere. Your application fee will not be refunded even if you decide to go to another school or not to go to school at all.

The application cost is relatively insignificant compared to your tuition fees but shouldn't be ignored when you budget for your upcoming college expenses.

CHOOSING YOUR EDUCATIONAL PROGRAM

You don't have much choice in the requirements for admission to your community college, but, once you're enrolled, the course of your study is up to you. To choose wisely, it's essential that you're familiar with the various programs and degrees your college offers and the career paths to which they lead.

Community colleges generally offer three categories of programs: transfer, nontransfer, and non-matriculated.

Transfer Programs

Transfer programs are designed to provide you with the foundations of your college career. As the name implies, they are constructed to facilitate transfer to a four-year school. If you complete the foundational courses at a community college, you can transfer to a four-year school and continue your study by taking upper-level courses.

The Associate of Arts Degree

The Associate of Arts (AA) degree is not a degree based only on art! It is a degree granted to students who have successfully completed a predominantly liberal arts and sciences program. AA degree programs are designed to provide students with a broad-based introduction to a wide range of disciplines. Your college will either prescribe certain courses within a specified range of disciplines or allow some leeway in the choice of classes within the disciplines. (We explain "core" and distribution requirements in greater detail in Chapter 6, "Before You Register Read This.")

Although the predominant AA degree is in Liberal Arts and Sciences, there are AA degrees in more specific areas as well. For example, your school might offer an AA in Criminal Justice. In this case, the program will offer a broad base of liberal arts and sciences classes but require specific courses in sociology and criminology as well.

An AA program generally comprises courses in

- Social sciences, which include courses in economics, sociology, anthropology, psychology, geography, and political science
- Humanities, which include courses in literature, history, art, music, theater, and communications
- Natural sciences, which include courses in biology, physics, chemistry, geology, and environmental studies
- Mathematics
- Foreign languages, which include courses in Spanish, French, Chinese, Korean, Hawaiian, Japanese, and Italian

DIGGING DEEPER

More and more community colleges are offering American Sign Language as a choice to satisfy their foreign language requirements.

The AA degree prepares students for a wide variety of careers. Many teachers, for example, receive their AA degree before continuing on for teacher certification from a four-year college. An AA degree in communications helps students prepare for careers in public relations, journalism, and media.

The AA degree (as well as the AS degree described in the next section) is geared for students who plan to go on to a four-year college where they will earn their Bachelor of Arts (BA) degree or, in some cases, a Bachelor of Science (BS).

DIGGING DEEPER

Many community colleges, aware that students may already have an interest in a particular field, offer an option along with the Liberal Arts and Sciences degree. You might, for instance, receive an AA in Liberal Arts and Sciences with a Music option. The Music option allows you to take anywhere from six to eighteen credits in the music specialization. Or the AA degree may be titled with the course of study. For example, Pima Community College in Arizona offers an AA in Anthropology, which allocates 31 credits in a broad-based course of study and 27 credits in anthropology.

The Associate of Science Degree

The Associate of Science (AS) degree is similar to the AA degree but, as the title implies, it focuses on training in areas that are connected to science or mathematics. Students who receive the AS degree generally transfer to a four-year college to receive their Bachelor of Science (BS) degree.

EXAMPLES OF ASSOCIATE OF ARTS DEGREES

Liberal Arts and Sciences	Liberal Studies
Teaching	American Sign Language Interpreting
Anthropology	Black Studies
Fine Arts	Dramatic Studies
English	Chicano Studies

An AS degree begins the preparation for numerous careers, including animation, aerospace engineering, farming and forestry, exercise science, new media, and zoology.

Many emerging technology industries require skills taught in the AS program. For example, if you're seeking a career as a systems analyst or programmer, you might consider pursuing an AS degree with a concentration in computer science.

As we mentioned previously, these divisions are fluid and differ from college to college. But here's what's essential to recognize: if you wish to transfer to a four-year college, you'll want to complete a full sixty or more credit AA or AS program.

EXAMPLES OF ASSOCIATE OF SCIENCE DEGREES

Liberal Arts and Sciences	Exercise and Sport Science
Chemistry	New Media Art
Biology	Accounting
Environmental Sciences	Information Technology
Math	Food Service
Business Administration	Geographic Information Systems

Nontransfer Programs

In addition to the transfer degrees, community colleges offer so-called and badly named "terminal" programs, or nontransfer programs, upon completion of which students generally seek employment immediately.

The Associate of Applied Science Degree and the Associate of Applied Arts Degree

The Associate of Applied Science (AAS) and the more infrequent Associate of Applied Arts (AAA) degree programs are designed to provide marketable skills you can bring directly to the workplace.

The choices in these programs are broad and continually growing. Students can earn their AAS in many different fields, from law enforcement administration to hospitality management. The AAA programs are primarily in the arts and include fine arts as well as commercial music. In these classes you can expect hands-on experience in your area of concentration.

If you decide to go for an AAS or AAA degree, your course of study will be narrower than if you were in an AA or AS program. You'll focus on the specific technical/occupational area you are studying and probably take no more than five to seven courses in the humanities and sciences. Many AAS programs require coursework to meet the mandate of industry agencies—for example, the Accreditation Review Committee on Education in Surgical Technology for the AAS degree in surgical technology.

Students who seek the terminal AAS or AAA degree intend to enter the job market upon receiving their degree and generally don't expect to transfer to four-year colleges, at least not immediately. Indeed, because of their specificity, many of the courses in the AAS and AAA programs don't transfer smoothly to four-year schools. However, schools are seeing that more and more students are continuing their study after receiving their AAS. So don't think that just because you will graduate with an AAS, this has to be the end of your education. It doesn't. Either after graduation or after some years in the workplace, you might want to explore the option of furthering your education—and furthering your career.

EXAMPLES OF ASSOCIATE OF APPLIED ARTS DEGREES (AAA)

Gallery Management	Fine Arts
Studio Arts	Interior Design
Commercial Music	Stage Technology

EXAMPLES OF ASSOCIATE OF APPLIED SCIENCE DEGREES (AAS)

Computer Assisted Drafting

Nursing

Office Administration and Technology

Paralegal Studies

Automotive Technology

Respiratory Care

Graphic Design

Dental Hygiene

Aviation Support

Millwright Technology

Occupational Studies

Office Administration and Technology

Nuclear Medicine Technology

Law Enforcement Administration

Fire Science

Ornamental Horticulture

Surgical Technology

Pharmaceutical Manufacturing

Agricultural Business Technology

Hospitality Management

Radiologic Technology

Construction and Facilities Support

Nuclear Technology

Marketing

Electrical–Mechanical Systems and Maintenance

Be aware that there are no hard and fast rules about these degree designations. For example, one college may offer a course of study in New Media as an AA while another school may list it as an AS and a third may even offer an AAS in the same area with basically the same courses.

Certificate Programs

Community colleges also offer credit-bearing classes for students who seek to develop specific skills for particular vocations. One might, for example, earn a certificate in medical transcription, translation and interpretation, or architectural drafting.

The aim of certification programs is to provide students with the vocational skills they'll need to begin working in their fields as soon as they complete their coursework. (Although these certificate programs are generally geared toward entry-level positions, in many cases they are very specialized higher-level programs that build on a student's education and experience. One such program is the Aquarium Science Certificate at Oregon Coast Community College, for which you need a BS in Life Science to apply.) To assist in this transition, many community colleges work directly with local companies and organizations in industries for which the college offers certificate programs. Certificate programs also prepare students for state or national examinations in various vocations. With certification you'll find preference in hiring and higher wages when you enter the job market in your field.

EXAMPLES OF CERTIFICATE PROGRAMS

Transportation, Warehousing, and Logistics Management

Family Violence Intervention

Landscape and Horticulture

Dental Assisting

Computer Aided Drafting (CAD)

Culinary Arts

Radio Frequency Identification Technology

Retail Management

The typical certificate program requires fewer credits than the two-year programs and generally can be completed in a year of full-time study (thirty credits or less). You might find a certificate program—for example, a Webmaster Certificate or Personal Trainer Certification—a good way to learn a skill that provides financial support while you continue your schooling. Certification is likely to land you with a better job than you'd obtain with only a high school degree, but it will not provide you with the breadth of education or training you'd receive with an AAS degree. At many community colleges, students can choose to study for an AA or AS degree in their chosen field after achieving their certification.

Non-Matriculated Programs

To receive any of the degrees or certificates described previously you must be a matriculated student—that is, accepted for admission to the college, registered in a curriculum, and taking credit-bearing courses toward a degree or certificate. But community colleges offer other avenues of study that are not directed to degrees or certification.

DIGGING DEEPER

Be aware that you may have to take more credits than a certificate program actually lists. That's because some courses require prerequisites that are not stated in the program description. Some schools will waive these prerequisites for students with equivalent knowledge and experience. But if you don't have the courses or their equivalents, you will need to meet this additional requirement.

Lifelong Learning/Continuing Education

Beyond credit-bearing courses, community colleges offer students a host of classes that teach everything from how to write a résumé to how to establish your own floral shop, attain a real estate license, sell insurance, or enter the health care industry. Formerly referred to as continuing education, these classes are now more popularly known as lifelong learning. These noncredit courses are usually short-term and have convenient schedules. They are also relatively inexpensive.

Another set of noncredit courses offered by community colleges covers basic skills for adults. These include English as a second language and high school equivalency classes for those who never graduated high school.

AND REMEMBER...

Once you have applied to college and submitted all the relevant documents on time, review the variety of paths your community college offers to professional careers and future education. In choosing the plan of study that best tracks your goals, keep these two truths in mind: (1) the more you know about these different programs the more intelligent your choice will be, and (2) your first choice need not be your only choice—you can change your mind later when a different career direction seems to better fit your interests.

To manage your money well while in community college, you'll need to appreciate the actual costs of school; learn about all the financial resources available, including grants, scholarships, and loans; and be diligent about completing and filing the appropriate applications and forms.

Money Matters

COMMUNITY COLLEGE is a smart investment. It is far less expensive than four-year colleges, and when you hit the job market, you'll recoup your tuition payments many times over. Nonetheless, the cost of a community college education is a serious challenge to many community college students who struggle to come up with the necessary funds each term.

In this chapter, we'll provide a no-nonsense, straightforward review of how you can better budget your college expenses and show you how you can get financial assistance to help pay your way through school.

Let's begin with the *expense* side of the equation—the actual cost of your community college education.

REAL COSTS OF COLLEGE

Your expenditures will fall into four broad categories:
- tuition
- fees

- books
- miscellaneous costs

Tuition

Tuition is the fee you pay to take classes. It is the bulk of your educational expenses. Most schools determine your tuition on the basis of cost per credit hour. Therefore, your tuition bill will depend on how many credits you take. Let's suppose you're registering for twelve credits in the coming semester: if your college charges $175 per credit hour, your tuition will be $2,100 for one semester. So, at this tuition rate, a full academic year of twelve credits for each of two semesters is $4,200.

A number of community colleges charge a flat fee that isn't based on credit hours. They may, for example, charge $2,400 for a semester or $4,800 for the year. A flat fee usually covers a range of credits (twelve to eighteen). There are, we should note, additional tuition fees for those taking an unusually heavy course load. And international students often pay per credit even if there is a flat fee for others.

When budgeting for college, find out at the outset which of these two ways your college computes tuition costs. But keep in mind that most financial aid awards do not cover summer school or intersession tuition.

DIGGING DEEPER

Do you live in the same state as your community college? State residents usually pay a lower rate than do out-of-state and international students. But some states have reciprocity agreements that allow residents of neighboring states to qualify for the in-state reduction. If this is your situation, find out if you qualify for this savings.

Fees

In addition to tuition, you will be charged for the use of college re-sources. Schools might have fees for use of technology, health services, labs, art studios, or other campus facilities. Colleges differ on how these fees are to be paid: some ask for a per-term payment to cover all fee requirements, and others charge on a per-use basis. In any case, don't be caught unaware. Though these fees are usually not exorbitant, you need to know what they are and budget accordingly.

Books

College students are often stunned at how much books can cost. If you haven't already been to the bookstore, you'll soon discover why they're so shocked. Prepare to pay hundreds of dollars each term on required textbooks. There are, however, strategies you can use to reduce this cost, and in Chapter 7, "Registration and Right After—Without Losing Your Mind," we'll suggest a few. Nonetheless, even with these savings, textbooks are pricey, so make sure to include this cost as you budget for the school year.

WHO WOULD'VE THOUGHT?

According to a study conducted by the Government Account-ability Office (GAO), over the past two decades, textbook prices have risen at twice the rate of annual inflation.[1]

Miscellaneous Costs

Life is expensive. In addition to your fixed tuition and fees, you'll have to budget for many other college-related costs. Here are some other possible expenditures:

- *Transportation:* You'll need to factor in automobile-related costs, like gas, maintenance, and parking. Or the cost of public trans-portation if that's how you'll get to and from school.

- *Technology:* If you don't have a computer, you'll need to get one. You might need to outlay money for software as well.
- *Child care:* This is a necessity for many community college students. If you have children, you will need to budget for the cost of child care while you're attending classes.
- *Clothes:* You'll be out of the house much of the time. You need to be dressed.
- *Food:* Now that you're constantly on the run, you might find yourself buying more food and spending more than you did eating at home.

This is just the short list. In addition, you should expect the unexpected and set aside some money for those financial demands that show up when you least expect them and, of course, when you can least afford them. Let's hope you get lucky and don't need to dip into this reserve at all.

FROM THE AUTHORS' FILES

One of the smartest things I figured out in college was how to use the school's facilities not only as learning resources but to save money. I still do that now as a professor. I take my laps in the school's pool and—when I conquer my laziness—take a run on the gym's treadmill. Why spend money at a private gym? I save money on books too; if the campus library doesn't have the one I want, they usually can get it from another library. The computer lab has software I need that's too expensive for me to purchase. And this year I plan to visit the music department to practice some piano during a free hour. All of these resources are available to students as well. What an easy way to save money! *JH*

PAYING FOR COLLEGE

The cost for college is considerable, but here's the brighter side of the equation: financial aid is available. Full-time students enrolled in public community college receive an average of about $2,000 in grants and tax benefits from the government as well as public and private sources![2]

WHO WOULD'VE THOUGHT?

About one-half of community college students receive some sort of financial aid.[3]

But this money won't simply be handed to you. To receive it, you'll need a solid understanding of how these funds are dispensed. You'll need to undertake research into potential funding sources, complete the applications, and submit the supporting materials—all before the deadlines. You've got work to do.

Knowing the Ground Rules

Financial aid resources for community college students are plentiful, and you'll be surprised by how many of these you qualify for. And there's more good news: nearly all the information you need is accessible online—legwork is now fingerwork on your computer keyboard.

Types of Financial Resources

To help you get started on your exploration, let's define the types of financial resources available to you.

- *Grants:* Grants are funds given to students that do not require repayment. Generally, grants are needs-based rather than merit-based. In other words, your eligibility will be determined not by your grades but by your financial circumstances. Other factors that may determine grant eligibility are your area of study, occupation, minority status, and state of residence.
- *Scholarships:* Scholarships, like grants, do not have to be repaid. But unlike grants, which are usually based on a student's financial need, scholarships are usually based on achievement. They are typically awarded to students with special skills, such as athletic

or artistic abilities, as well as academic accomplishments. Your research will point you to the few scholarships that are needs-based as well.

- *Work–study programs:* The federal government has designated money for students who work at specified jobs (often tied to campus responsibilities). Community colleges sometimes offer their own work–study programs. Because this money is earned, it need not be repaid.

- *Loans:* Loans are funds you borrow from either the federal or state government or a private institution such as a bank. Loans need to be repaid with interest. Government-issued student loans tend to have the lowest interest rate and the best terms for repayment. There are, in addition, deferred payment programs that issue loans to pay for tuition and fees and do not charge interest.

The All-Important FAFSA

Before we look in greater detail at these different types of financial assistance, we need to turn our attention to the Free Application for Federal Student Aid, known as FAFSA. Students rely on this form for all federal grants, loans, and work–study funding, and most states and schools use FAFSA information to determine their own financial awards. It's vital, therefore, that you become familiar with this widely used application at the outset.

As most government grants use FAFSA, this is the only form you'll need to complete, and you can submit the form either online or on paper. Either way, complete it carefully. For introductory instructions on how to fill out this form, visit the FAFSA site at http://studentaid.ed.gov/students/attachments/siteresources/CompletingtheFAFSA07-08.pdf.

The government analyzes your FAFSA application to determine whether you're entitled to a grant and how much money you're entitled to. It considers the tuition you need to pay against your family income, the contribution you can make toward your tuition. If, for argument's sake, the cost of attendance at school is $2,000, and you can reasonably pay $500, your grant will be $1,500. This determination of how much you can reasonably provide toward tuition is your Expected Family Contribution, or EFC.

Four to six weeks after you submit your FAFSA, you'll receive your

Student Aid Report (SAR) by e-mail or regular mail. This report details your EFC, the amount the government has determined your family will be asked to contribute toward your education. Make sure you review your Student Aid Report to ensure that all of your submitted information is accurate. (Note: If you or your family has special circumstances that will affect your financial situation, such as unusual medical or dental expenses or a significant change in income between last year and the present year, contact your school's financial aid office to discuss your special situation.) For more information about the EFC go to http://www.studentaid.ed.gov/students/publications/student_guide/index.html.

CHECKLIST FOR FILING YOUR FAFSA

- Read the instructions carefully. Words like "household," "household income," "investments," and "dependents" have specific meanings here.
- Complete your tax return before filling out your FAFSA (if you are a dependent student, have your parents complete their tax return if possible). You'll need this information. You can still apply for the FAFSA if you haven't yet filed your tax return, but you'll need to provide that data if you are to receive a grant.
- Plan ahead. Gather information like your Social Security number, driver's license number, income tax return, and investment records before you begin. The FAFSA site provides a list of documentation you will need. It also provides a list of eligibility requirements (citizenship status, high school diploma or equivalency, and so on).
- Be diligent in answering questions. It's easy to make mistakes; computing adjusted gross income (AGI) and total income tax and completing worksheets can be complicated. Mistakes can delay the processing of your application. FastWeb's College Gold provides a list of common errors at http://www.collegegold.com/applydecide/commonfafsaerrors. There are also sites that offer free professional help filling out the FAFSA form, such as College Goal Sunday at http://www.collegegoalsundayusa.org.
- File electronically! It's a lot faster. The FAFSA on the Web Worksheet is designed so that you can enter information and save your work

for weeks before sending off your completed application. No wonder over 90 percent of the FAFSA applications are submitted online! Make sure to keep a copy of your filing. The Web site for filing is http://www.fafsa.ed.gov.

- Check the status of your application on the FAFSA home page at http://www.fafsa.ed.gov./FOTWWebApp/follow003.jsp. Click on the link "Check Status of a Submitted FAFSA."

Residency Requirements

In most cases, you need to be a U.S. citizen to apply for federal financial aid. The FAFSA form asks specific questions about your state residency, such as where you live and where your parents live. You will also be asked to note whether you are classified as a dependent or independent. To learn about state residency requirements for FAFSA, check out the Department of Education's page on application questions at http://studentaid.ed.gov/students/publications/completing_fafsa/2007_2008/ques2-1.html. This site is updated every year.

WHO WOULD'VE THOUGHT?

In a recent national survey of community college students, only 56 percent had even completed the FAFSA. Of those who had not, 38 percent felt they did not qualify for financial aid, but another 18 percent had no reason.[4] Don't be one of those who lose out.

Financial Resources

Now that you're dealing (or have already dealt) with your FAFSA, let's take a closer look at the potential resources for financial aid we mentioned previously.

Grants

FEDERAL GRANTS

The federal government in Washington, D.C., is the largest dispenser of grants to students. These grants help pay for tuition, books, supplies (including computer and computer access), living expenses, and dependent care. *Applying for a federal grant is your first priority.*

You'll be pleased to discover how relatively easy the feds have made the application process. Begin with a visit to the Student Aid on the Web page at http://www.studentaid.ed.gov. Here you'll learn about your eligibility for the various government grant programs. But remember, while financial need is the main criterion for grant eligibility, it's not the only one; your special needs and interests might be a factor as well. And bear in mind that eligibility for grants and the amount of money distributed are constantly revised, so even if you don't qualify one semester, you might qualify in a later semester.

PELL GRANTS

The main federal grant to community college students is called the Pell Grant. The Pell Grant is needs-based and determined by consideration of your financial requirements only, not your grade point average (GPA) or other achievements. After your FAFSA is submitted, your college can quickly determine whether you are eligible for a Pell Grant.

WHO WOULD'VE THOUGHT?

Pell Grants are named for Claiborne Pell who represented Rhode Island in the U.S. Senate from 1961 to 1997 and is largely responsible for the creation of these grants.

How much money will you receive from a federal Pell Grant? The amount varies from student to student and depends partially on the cost of tuition and your EFC (described previously in the description of the FAFSA application): the lower your EFC, the larger the grant.

Here are a few tips on how to lower the value of your calculated assets and thereby lower your EFC:

- If you have investments like stocks and bonds, explore the possibility of transferring them to your grandparents' name.
- If you are planning on making a big purchase (a car, say), make your purchase before filling out the FAFSA. This way, your application does not show excess cash in your bank account.
- The government allows greater allowances for households with more than one student attending college. If this applies to you, make sure to note it in your application.

Pell Grants are only awarded to undergraduate students who have not earned a bachelor's or professional degree. Community college students increasingly rely on Pell Grants to help them pay their way through college.[5]

OTHER FEDERAL GRANTS

Pell Grants are the leading federal student grants, but not the only ones. Another is the Federal Supplemental Educational Opportunity Grant (FSEOG). The FSEOG Program provides needs-based grants to low-income undergraduate students with priority given to students with "exceptional need," those with the lowest expected family contributions, as computed by—you guessed it—the FAFSA. You can receive an FSEOG *in addition* to a Pell Grant. And the good news is that you do not have to complete any additional forms to file for this grant—your application is automatically reviewed once your FAFSA is completed. You can learn more about the grant at http://www.fseog.com.

STATE GRANTS

State grants, like federal grants, are typically needs based. Your completed FAFSA will usually be sufficient to determine your eligibility for a state grant. As state grants are often less strict in calculating your income, you could qualify for state aid even if you've been denied a federal grant.

A number of states offer Tuition Assistance Program (TAP) grants. TAP awards can be as high as $5,000 per year and are worth investigating. States also offer grants to special populations such as the unemployed, individuals in need of special medical care, and persons with disabilities (circumstances that are not always considered in federal grants).

Consult your state's Department of Education Web site for information on how to apply for these various state grants. These grants often have credit requirements (such as full-time status), pursuit of progress requirements (completion of a certain number of credits each semester), and GPA requirements.

Scholarships

Scholarships come in all sizes and from a wide range of sources. To find out about scholarship possibilities, have a conversation with the personnel at the financial aid office at the college. They can answer many of your questions and point you in directions you might not have otherwise considered. They'll also save you valuable time by pointing out which avenues of your queries are dead ends. (If you're a high school senior, make sure to discuss scholarships with your high school's college counselor.)

Your school can provide a directory of potential scholarship sources, but to make sure you haven't neglected a different scholarship for which you might qualify, *conduct your own research*. Many students wrongly assume that to earn a scholarship for college, they need to have a brilliant academic record or demonstrate extraordinary athletic or artistic talent. Sometimes what matters most is that you're persistent!

As you begin your research into available scholarships, you'll come across lists of government scholarships, but don't stop your search with those lists. There are numerous, less-publicized scholarships for which you might qualify. CollegeData, at https://www.collegedata. com/cs/search/scholar/scholar_search_tmpl.jhtml, is a Web site with a remarkable scholarship finder. On this site, you can enter your GPA, ethnicity, course of study, and any identifying talent or characteristic, and a list of scholarships for which you are eligible appears. So, for example, if you're a Hispanic American majoring in film with a GPA of 2.5, plugging in this information will produce a list of scholarships for individuals with this profile. If, say, you have the above characteristics and also have a family member who was in the Armed Services, you'll find additional scholarship opportunities. There are over 450,000 scholarships awarded to American students each year. Some have your name on them, but you won't know unless you seek them out.

CHECKLIST OF SCHOLARSHIP RESOURCES

- *Your college.* Colleges often designate scholarships for students who bring to the school superior academic achievement or special talents in art, music, or sports.
- *Religious organizations.* Your local house of worship might have a scholarship fund for promising students.
- *Minority-membership scholarships.* There are scholarships designated for community college students from minority groups. The Hispanic Scholarship Fund, for example, provides scholarships to Hispanic high school students planning to attend college and Hispanic community college students planning to transfer to a four-year college.
- *Community organizations and civic groups.* These organizations often award scholarships for worthy students.
- *Organizations related to your field of interest.* The American Medical Association and American Bar Association, for example, provide scholarships to students interested in pursuing careers in these respective fields, as do many other professional organizations.
- *Unions.* Your union or your parents' union might have scholarships or tuition plans for which you might qualify.
- *Honor societies.* Phi Theta Kappa, the international honor society of the two-year college, is perhaps the best-known of honor societies that provide scholarships to high-achieving college students.
- *Foundations.* Many foundations provide student scholarships for which you might be eligible. Some are corporate foundations such as Coca-Cola, which provides the Coca-Cola Two-Year College Scholarship; others are private, such as the Jack Kent Cooke Foundation, which awards up to $30,000 per year to qualifying students.

One last note: keep your eyes peeled for the unusual scholarship that could well be a financial resource for you. For example, if you like skateboarding and have a good GPA, you might be able to receive $5,000 from the Patrick Kerr Skateboard Scholarship. If you are a tall male or female, you might want to try for the Tall Clubs International Scholarship. If you have promoted vegetarianism in your school or community, you can apply for the Vegetarian Resource Group Scholarship of up to $10,000. If your last name is Van Valkenburg or a variation, you are really in luck: you can receive $1,000 from the Van Valkenburg Memorial Scholarship. And if you have always been into duct tape, there is money out there for you as well. The Duck Brand Duct Tape Stuck on Prom Contest awards a $6,000 scholarship to the couple who makes their own prom outfits out of duct tape. When we say there are scholarships out there for you, we are NOT joking!

You should also visit the reference section of your local library. Ask for a copy of the most recent guide to foundations, and note the description and contact for scholarships for which you might be eligible.

Applying for a scholarship is not a one-time event, available to you only when entering college. You can be awarded a scholarship at many different points in your college career. So be certain to check in periodically with the financial aid office at your college.

DIGGING DEEPER

Be suspicious of organizations that charge a fee to submit your application for a scholarship. Some are genuine, but many are scams; generally, you can receive the same information you'll get from these sites from your school or the U.S. Department of Education at no cost. In addition, there are first-rate sites that provide resources for thousands of scholarships. FastWeb, at http://www.fastweb.com, and FinAid, at http://www.finaid.org, are two such sites. Be especially wary if the scholarship sponsor doesn't offer contact information such as an e-mail address, mailing address (a P.O. box is not good enough), or phone number. Don't believe you've been awarded a scholarship for which you didn't apply, and don't be fooled by official-looking seals or official-sounding names that include words like "national" or "federal." Always investigate the source offering the scholarship.

Work–Study Programs

One way to have enough money for college is to work for it. Work–study programs offer part-time jobs for college students to help them earn income while attending school. Because you work for this money, it need not be repaid.

Many work–study opportunities are funded by the federal government. These jobs are right there on campus or at a nearby off-campus not-for-profit organization. The pay is at least the current hourly minimum and paid to you by the college. But be aware that the federal work–study award only provides limited hours, and the amount of the compensation depends primarily on your financial need.

Community colleges often offer their own work–study programs. Find out if yours does and what qualifications you need to participate.

Loans

What if the grants or scholarships don't come through, and you haven't been able to attain a work–study grant? Or suppose you have been awarded some money but not enough? If you need more funding to pay for college, what are your options now? Consider a loan.

DIGGING DEEPER

One way you *don't* want to pay for what you need in college is with a credit card. Some 75 percent of college students have credit cards now—up from 67 percent in 1998—and they're piling up debt. Suppose you have a $500 card balance at the average interest rate of 16 percent. If you make only minimum payments, it'll take you more than three years to pay off what you owe. You might need a single card for emergencies, but be careful—financial mistakes made in college can haunt you long after graduation. Credit scores have an impact on employment, qualifications for renting or buying an apartment, future loans, and much more.

But from whom? Of course, you can sometimes get private loans, but your first and best resource is the federal government. Federal student loans are the easiest public loans to obtain and have the most flexible repayment schedules, and the lowest interest rates. To be eligible for a federal loan you must be at least a part-time student at a qualified school. The loans are paid directly to your college to cover your school fees.

The first step for getting *any* federal loan is something you've already done in applying for a grant or scholarship—completing and submitting the FAFSA.

The following are among the most important federal government loans.

PERKINS LOANS

The Perkins Loan is designated for students with exceptional needs. The U.S. Department of Education provides a designated amount of funding to the school, and the school, in turn, determines which students have the greatest need. The college will combine federal funds with some of its own funds for loans to qualifying students.

This loan is a subsidized loan, which means that you will not have to pay back any of it while you are in school or during the nine-month grace period following graduation. The government pays the interest that accumulates while you are in school.

If you need to take out a loan, the Perkins is considered the best because (1) the interest rate is the lowest, (2) you don't have to pay it back until nine months after you have graduated, (3) it has significantly higher loan limits than other federal loans, and (4) you have ten years to fully repay the money.

WHO WOULD'VE THOUGHT?

Perkins loans are named for Congressman Carl D. Perkins from the seventh Congressional District of Kentucky, a strong advocate of student aid programs, including federal scholarships, work study, and student loans.

STAFFORD LOANS

A Stafford Loan is a federal student loan that is either subsidized like the Perkins or unsubsidized. An unsubsidized loan is not based on financial need, and the government does not pay the interest while you

are in school. No matter how much your family earns and how substantial your assets, you qualify for an unsubsidized Federal Stafford
Loan.

WHO WOULD'VE THOUGHT?

In 1988, the Federal Guaranteed Student Loan Program was
renamed the Robert T. Stafford Student Loan Program in honor
of Vermont's Senator Robert Stafford for his work in higher
education.

The benefits of the Federal Stafford Loan Program are attractive interest rates and deferred payments (although the Perkins Loan interest
rates and repayment terms are still better).

There are other federal loans besides the Perkins and Stafford. To learn
about these other possible resources, research the government education
Web site at http://www.ed.gov/finaid/info/find/edpicks.jhtml?src=ov, and
speak to the people in the financial office of your college.

DEFERRED PAYMENT PROGRAMS

Most community colleges offer deferred payment programs (these
have various names) that allow students to pay the balance of their
tuition fees—interest free—in several installments over the period of
the semester. Some of these programs are managed by the college itself; others are managed through third parties such as TuitionPay Plan.
The only cost to you is a small enrollment fee of usually $25 to $50 per
semester. Apply for this service early; don't wait until registration day.

APPLICATIONS AND DEADLINES

We cannot overstate the importance of accurate completion of the
forms and strict adherence to the deadlines when applying for any
financial assistance. If you neglect to fill out the required forms accurately and completely, you'll delay receipt of your funding or not
receive it at all.

These application forms can be complicated, so don't hesitate to get help. The sites we've mentioned previously are good places for this assistance.

Details matter in these forms. When completing the FAFSA, for example, pay attention to which questions you leave blank. If, say, you're a U.S. citizen, you wouldn't answer the question referring to your Alien Registration Number. However, check the "no" box to the question "Are you a male?" even if you think it's obvious from your name or other information you've noted that you're a female. Complete and accurate answers are crucial.

Receiving Your Money

You might be wondering when you'll get your government money if you've been awarded a financial stipend or loan. The answer is just about never. Only a small portion, if any, of federal scholarships, grants, and loans goes directly to you. Financial aid is paid to you through your school. Typically, the college first uses the funds to pay tuition and fees, and the remaining money is returned to you for your other expenses.

AND REMEMBER...

Paying for college is a serious financial challenge. The expenses are considerable and constant. But, as you learned from this chapter, help is out there. Tens of billions of dollars are issued to students every year in the form of grants, scholarships, and loans. *And millions of dollars available for college students go unclaimed!* Applying for funds takes time and effort. But if you're committed to your education, your diligence will be repaid many times over.

Adult students face many obstacles as they begin or return to college, but by learning key strategies for achieving academic success, you can overcome these hurdles and have a rewarding college experience.

Cheers for the Adult Student

IF YOU'RE AN ADULT BEGINNING or returning to college, with more than a couple of years between you and your high school years, the challenge might seem overwhelming, even frightening. But millions of adults undertake this challenge each year and succeed. In fact, half the students now enrolled in higher education are twenty-five years old and older.[1]

WHO WOULD'VE THOUGHT?

In a 2006 national study of Americans ages twenty-five to sixty, more than half indicated they'd like to pursue additional education.[2]

And where are these adults turning to get their education? Millions are choosing community college.

So if you, too, are an adult student in community college, have a look around your classroom. You're bound to notice that you aren't the only person in the room with life experience and a determination to improve your life.

A GOOD FIT—WITH MAYBE A BUMP ALONG THE WAY

Adult students enroll at community colleges for a variety of reasons. Some return to further their educational goals, others seek a degree or certification to advance in their chosen careers, and others have decided to pursue new careers entirely.

Benefits

Why do many adults choose community college?

WHO WOULD'VE THOUGHT?

More than one million baby boomers are enrolled in the nation's 1,200 community colleges to retool for their next careers, according to the American Association of Community Colleges. College administrators expect millions more to follow in the immediate years ahead.

For one thing, money concerns are especially serious for adults, and community colleges are a lot less expensive than four-year colleges. Second, travel time adds up, and the easier access to the local community colleges is an important benefit for adults who are already pressed for time meeting their work and family obligations. The flexible hours at community colleges—courses given at night and weekends—allow adults to attend school when they otherwise could not.

And beyond convenience, many adult students are more likely to flourish in a community college setting than in a traditional four-year college. These students generally perform better in learning environments that combine lectures with discussion than they do in the more typical pure-lecture settings of four-year schools, and they often receive more direct support for their needs as well.[4]

Challenges

The benefits of community college for adult students are significant, but so are the challenges they face.

Psychological Hurdles

Your decision to return to school takes resolve and courage. True, there are likely to be other adults in your classroom; nonetheless, you're in a distinct minority. Twenty-nine might be the average age of community college students, but many of your classmates will be in their younger twenties, and quite a few will still be in their late teens. It's not unreasonable for an older student to feel a bit out of place in this environment. So you may find yourself hit with a flurry of doubts:

- I've been out of school too long.
- I won't have the time to study and keep up with my assignments.
- Even if I once had the necessary skills, now they're gone.
- I'll never fit in.

There's more. You wonder if you have the stamina to complete all your school work. Are you capable of pulling off all-nighters, cramming for tests, and completing papers? You're not sure you're prepared to deal again with having your work graded. And you wonder if it really makes sense to take this much time away from your family and friends.

We're certain, however, that these worries can be overcome and that your decision to attend college is a wise one. Let's have a look, then, at how you can overcome these obstacles.

Academic Concerns

One persistent fear of adult students is that they lack the academic skills to succeed in college. Perhaps this finding will lessen some of that worry: a history of solid research demonstrates that *adult students earn better grades than younger students!*[3] This is true across all majors. Why this is so is a matter of controversy among educators, but what is not debatable is that you, the adult student, bring distinctive advantages to your classes and studies. These include a higher level of maturity, a greater readiness to learn, and life experiences that help you make sense of the material you study. And, as an adult, you approach your career objectives not as an abstraction but an immediate, practical goal.

Not only do adult students do better in their classes than younger students, but the performance of younger students improves when in the presence of older students. So not only are you likely to perform as well or better than the younger students in your class, but your being there helps them do better as well. Having mature adults in the classroom encourages classmates and instructors to work harder.

FROM THE AUTHORS' FILES

Fifteen years ago, I had a lovely thirty-eight-year-old woman in my Public Speaking class. A divorced mother of three, she was an excellent student, but it didn't come easy to her. She really worked hard. Her dedication to the class was evident to other students. Whenever there was small group work, she guided her colleagues and kept them laughing—she had a great sense of humor. She received an A from me and went on her way. Recently, I saw her walking on campus. I enthusiastically asked her how she was doing, what was going on in her life, and what she was doing on campus. She told me she had gone on to complete her master's and doctoral degrees and had recently been hired as a faculty member at the school. I thought of the novelist George Eliot, who wrote, "It is never too late to be what you might have been." *DG*

BUT IF YOU BECOME FRUSTRATED...

Adult students can be easily flustered when they confront material difficult to understand or when they receive poor grades on an exam. Mistakenly, they attribute this disappointing performance to their age. Don't fall into this trap. Everyone hits an unpleasant patch in school, and age is not the reason.

If you find yourself beginning to despair and think you aren't cut out for college, remind yourself of your abilities and the courage you showed in deciding to enroll in college. The occasional pep talk can prove very helpful in keeping you on course when your determination begins to flag.

Financial Pressures

As we highlighted in the previous chapter, money matters to community college students. This is especially so for adult students who face not only paying for food and rent but often other expenses such as the costs of their children's education and taking care of aging parents. Getting your degree or certificate will prove to be a smart financial move. In the meantime, however, you need to make ends meet.

Here are several resources to investigate and some steps to take that can help you meet your financial needs.

GET YOUR COMPANY TO HELP WITH YOUR TUITION

If you are employed by a company, find out if you're entitled to receiving financial assistance for your education. About half of all major corporations have full reimbursement programs for college tuition, and many others will pick up at least part of the cost. In particular, investigate whether you can receive a Corporate Tuition Assistance Plan, a program designed to benefit employees who choose to further their education.[5]

RESEARCH SCHOLARSHIP POSSIBILITIES

Beyond the many scholarships available for all community college students, there are scholarships earmarked for returning adult students, and many of these are designated for adult women students and adult students from minority groups. Many of these scholarships are from private sources that are not publicly advertised such as professional organizations, churches, clubs, and other interest groups. Investigate whether you qualify for one.

PART-TIME STUDENTS HAVE RESOURCES, TOO

Most adult community college students have full-time jobs and are in school part time. As part-timers they are disqualified from receiving many types of financial aid and scholarships. Many, but not all. Each year new financial aid packages are announced, including loans and scholarships for which even part-timers are eligible. If you're going to school part time, you'll need to spend some time and effort discovering these resources. But it will be time and effort well invested.

YOUR STUDENT HEALTH INSURANCE POLICIES AND MEDICAL HELP

Medical insurance is prohibitively expensive for many. If you re-signed from a full-time job to enroll in school, you'll certainly miss the medical insurance that might have been part of your salary. However, your status as a student can ease some of the financial burden. Check out the health insurance available to you at the college and compare that cost with your own plan. Often, the college's plan is significantly cheaper. Seeing a doctor on campus rather than on your own—if your school provides this service—will save you considerable money.

You can also save money by taking the various vaccinations and medical tests that are widely available on campus to students. These range from tests for diabetes and high blood pressure to flu shots and mammograms. But avoid the temptation to proceed without insurance altogether. One illness or accident could be financially devastating if you're uninsured.

BUDGET REALISTICALLY

Now that you're back in school, you should begin budgeting not in terms of weeks or months but in terms of semesters. Your paychecks might continue to arrive every two weeks and your bills every month, but your school expenses are on a different schedule. Be careful not to exhaust your available funds during the first weeks of the semester: the financial aid checks you may receive at the beginning of the term must cover your school expenses through the end of the term.

STRATEGIES TO EASE THE REENTRY INTO SCHOOL

As we've been noting, adults face pressing challenges in returning to school. Here are eight strategies to ease the reentry.

Take It Slow in the Beginning

As an adult student, you might be in a rush to complete all your coursework. Believing it's already late in the game for you, you register for too many classes only to find yourself overextended and overwhelmed by the amount of work required. Many adult students overload themselves with classes and end up quitting school entirely. They convince themselves that they lack the staying power to complete their education, when in reality anyone, regardless of age, can be weighed down by a glut of classes.

Be realistic. You've been away from a school environment for some time, and it might take time to readapt. Consider beginning with fewer classes. This way you can acquaint yourself with school and reacquaint yourself with you, the student. You'll also better gauge how much time you can devote to your classwork and still handle your other commitments. As a result, you're less likely to burn out.

Consider a Summer School Class

While we're on the subject of scheduling, consider taking a class or two during the summer. And not just any class: take the one you've been avoiding. You worried that this class will prove extremely difficult and the work required will undermine your effort in your other classes. Enrolling for the course during the summer might be the perfect solution. As this will be your only class (or one of two), you'll be able to focus on it to a degree you couldn't during the regular school year. And consider this, too: because it's a concentrated summer course, you'll have to double your studying, but you'll also be done with it in a matter of weeks rather than months.

Determine When and Where You Do Your Best Studying

Are you most efficient studying at night or during the day? Do you prefer background noise or absolute silence? Do you prefer to be alone or in a place where others are studying, such as the library? Here's the kicker: you might not know the answer. As we will discuss in more detail in Chapter 12, "The ABCs of Getting As," many students think they know how they study best but get it wrong. This is a common problem, especially for adult students who rely on their previous history in school. What might have been true years earlier when you were in high school may no longer be the case today.

So experiment. Try out different settings and different hours. Be brutally honest as you discover your optimum learning environment and, as a result, save hundreds of hours of study time and improve your grades as well.

The next step is to let everyone around you know what you've concluded. Tell your family and friends and anyone else who might interfere: this is your study space, and this is your study time. You are not to be disturbed. Expect to be intruded upon at first, but remain adamant, and soon the people around you will get the idea and leave you alone.

STUDY TIPS FOR ADULTS

- Create workable routines. Decide on a study time that works well with your existing schedule. Set aside a period each day for studying, and try to restrict these sessions to the same place and time.
- Make lists. Whenever you receive a new assignment or test date, write it down. You've got a lot on your plate—a host of commitments and appointments—and your school assignments can easily get lost in that confusion. Writing things down helps.
- Don't fall behind on your schoolwork. Keep up with your reading assignments and preparation for papers and exams throughout the term. Given your busy life, you probably won't have the luxury of a large block of time to complete a paper or prepare for an exam. So when given an assignment or test date, determine what you need to have done by when, and break down the task into small, manageable steps. Complete them day after day.
- Keep your school-material area uncluttered. This is difficult in a busy family environment, but demonstrating your own respect for your work quarters will help your children develop respect for their own study space.

Remember: Perfect Is the Enemy of the Good

Adult students are often the most grade conscious of all students. Worried about their capacity to return to school successfully, they're especially sensitive to their professors' evaluations. Don't make the mistake of setting up unrealistic expectations for yourself. No one will be perfect in every class. Telling yourself that nothing short of perfect grades is acceptable is a sure recipe for frustration and paralysis—and lower grades as a result.

Do keep your standards high. Do push yourself. Do perform at the highest level you can. And then let it be.

Be Kind to Your Body, Too

Going back to school makes demands on the adult student's body as well as on his or her mind. You're likely to find yourself rushing from place to place, eating poorly, and sleeping less. The stress can take its toll on your general well-being. Therefore:

Make sure you allow some time for breaks between classes. Use those minutes to eat, find a quiet corner and shut your eyes, go for a walk—whatever works to relax you.

Get sufficient sleep. We understand this isn't always an option for adult students, but try to make it a priority. Sleep deprivation has a significantly unfavorable impact on learning, and this is especially true for people as they age.

Stay in physical shape. Of course you wish you can. But there are resources on campus to help make this wish come true more easily than you might first imagine. As an enrolled student, you're eligible to use the gym at the college or swim in the pool if there is one, and all for free. What an inexpensive and fun way to stay in shape!

Participate in Classroom Discussions

As an adult student, you might be reluctant to participate in the back-and-forth of classroom exchanges. With the class dominated by younger people, you might feel like an outsider and think your perspective will not be appreciated. On the contrary, both your fellow students and your professors will appreciate your insights, and they will be a valuable contribution to the class discussion.

Active participation in the classroom is also extremely helpful to your own academic success. If you, like many adult students, work and have family obligations, the classroom may serve as your most active intellectual meeting place. So overcome your reservations and speak up.

Get to Know Your Professors

Developing a genuine relationship with your teacher is an important aspect of success in college. As we will see in Chapter 8, "Classified Intelligence for the Classroom," this is true for all students, but especially for adult students. You have a head start here. After all, you and many of your professors share something in common: you are the adults in the room. You all have experience under your belt and often have lived through the same times. Your professor will be interested in what you have to say, and by talking with your professor, you'll learn more in return.

Get Credit for Your Experience

You will, of course, lean on your experience as you make your way through your classes, but you might also be able to use your experience in a practical way. Many colleges do not offer credit for prior life and work experiences, but some do. If you've completed a corporate training seminar, received a license or certification, or been the author or creator of anything from a software program to a book, you might be eligible for credit. Organizations such as ACE's College Credit Recommendation Service (CREDIT) (visit http://www.acenet.edu/AM/Template.cfm?Section=CCRS) connect workplace learning with colleges and universities. You can use this service to gain academic credit for formal courses and examinations taken outside traditional degree programs. If you've been in the military, have a look at Defense Activity for Non-Traditional Education Support (DANTES) at http://www.dantes.doded.mil/Dantes_web/DANTESHOME.asp. This program offers advice on how to get credit for training you received in the military, such as technical skills, leadership skills, or skills in a foreign language, art, or geography.

DIGGING DEEPER

The College-Level Examination Program (CLEP) is a test developed by the College Entrance Examination Board to measure general educational knowledge and understanding of basic facts. CLEP is a national system of granting credit by examination. According to the College Board, there are 2,900 colleges that grant credit and/or advanced standing for CLEP exams. You can take an exam in a broad range of subjects in the humanities, college math and English, foreign languages, science, and business. To learn more about CLEP and the possibility of receiving credit for what you already know, visit the CLEP Web site at http://www.collegeboard.com/student/testing/clep/about.html.

In addition to your life and work experience, you may also have previous college credits/experience that can be applied to your new college career. Did you take classes in college way back when? Don't assume that you can't get credit for them, even if more than a decade has passed. Find out your college's policy on the acceptable time frame for obtaining credit for previous classes.

AND REMEMBER...

If no one has yet congratulated you for your bravery in returning to college, let us be the first to do so. Your decision is courageous, a clear statement of your belief in yourself and your ability to move ahead with your life. The key to achieving your goals is to dislodge yourself from old assumptions about what you can and cannot accomplish. This is a new beginning, full with new possibilities. Go forth and conquer!

Community college classes for students for whom English is a second language or who are in need of improvement in basic academic skills should be welcomed as useful opportunities to help you flourish in your college studies.

ESL and Remediation: Not Just for Beginners

MANY COMMUNITY COLLEGE STUDENTS are enrolled in English as a second language or remedial classes and view this as some sort of defect in their abilities. This discomfort is unwarranted. It's important to recognize that if English is your second language, you're among a minority of college students who are bilingual. This is a distinctive advantage in our contemporary global economy, in which mastery of multiple languages (and cultures) is a growing necessity. Nor should you feel any sense of deficiency because you've been told to take a remedial class. You're not alone; at least half of community college students are assigned to remedial classes.[1] Approach these remedial classes as a wonderful opportunity to get up to speed.

ENGLISH AS A SECOND LANGUAGE (ESL)

With so many foreign-born students, it's no surprise that community colleges have become central places for the millions of these students who need to develop their English reading, writing, and speaking skills. For example, ESL is the largest and fastest-growing program offered at Miami Dade College, and the ESL program at Santa Monica College is currently the largest ESL program in the world.

As an ESL student you are very much part of the college program, a full-fledged participant in your school.

You'll also discover the distinct advantages in taking ESL classes at a community college rather than in other institutions, including four-year colleges. One significant advantage is smaller class size. This results in more individualized attention, the extra consideration so beneficial when learning a language. Smaller classes also foster a more cooperative and supportive environment, which is particularly important to international students as they begin their American education.

Who Takes ESL Classes?

Community colleges offer ESL courses to international students who've taken the Test of English as a Foreign Language (TOEFL) and whose test score indicates that these classes are needed. Some colleges administer a state, city, or college-specific English proficiency exam, which also helps identify the need for the class. No matter what you score on these tests, your college will provide a level of study to meet your specific needs.

There is no typical ESL student. Adult English language learners represent a wide range of cultural and educational backgrounds and enroll in community college for a broad array of reasons. Some are eager to begin an associate's program but will benefit from greater proficiency in English. Other ESL students may not be enrolled in a full-time program of study but seek to improve their English to advance in their careers and jobs. Still others may have gone to college in their own country and even possess a degree but now are looking to make a new start with a new career in a new country and need to be fluent in English. No matter what your reason for taking ESL classes, you can be sure you will find like-minded classmates who share the same challenges.

Challenges

The focus of ESL classes is to help you improve your English language abilities. This includes reading comprehension, writing, grammar, vocabulary, speaking, pronunciation, and listening. Studies indicate that, of these language skills, ESL students find writing the most difficult to master.[2]

DIGGING DEEPER

Most native English speakers don't realize just how confounding learning English can be. How, for example, would you explain the rule for pronunciation and spelling of the sound that is underlined in the following words: jury, age, judge, soldier, procedure?

But as important as the academic challenges are the psychological obstacles you'll need to overcome if you are to succeed in ESL. The two most common of these hurdles are fear and embarrassment.

The fear factor is understandable: learning any new language is difficult, especially for adults. Moreover, ESL students face the added pressure of spending much of their days in environments—school, work, or the marketplace—where a facility with English is expected.

Embarrassment is another key barrier ESL students must overcome. Many—perhaps most—students for whom English is a second language are reluctant to exhibit their inability to speak or read fluently in their new language. This self-consciousness can be especially paralyzing for those who were born in the United States or have been in the country for some time and still need to improve their basic English skills.

Fear and embarrassment are genuine but not insurmountable challenges. It helps to recognize that most individuals in your ESL class are undergoing the same experience. It helps to remember, too, that most of us ourselves have confronted these fears and embarrassments or had parents, grandparents, and ancestors who did. They succeeded, and so will you.

FROM THE AUTHORS' FILES

My Eastern European immigrant parents always had a problem distinguishing between a "w" and a "v" when they spoke. But over the years, they worked hard on their English and soon displayed a richer vocabulary than their native-born American children. I think of their commitment to mastering their new language when I discuss ESL with my students. "Of course it's a battle," I acknowledge. "But keep at it, and your English will flourish." This isn't just empty pep talk. I've seen firsthand the embarrassment but also the achievement that awaits those who make the effort. *JH*

The best way to face up to fear and embarrassment is to meet the challenge head-on. Proficiency comes with practice. Try to place yourself in an English language environment whenever possible. Read English books and magazines. Listen to English radio, and watch English television. Speak English even if, at first, this makes you uncomfortable. If your children speak English better than you, delight in their ability and learn from them. But never fall back on your mother tongue out of fear or embarrassment. As you push on with your English, the cause of your discomfort will soon disappear.

WHO WOULD'VE THOUGHT?

Although you may think English is difficult to learn, there are many other languages that linguists consider even more difficult. Take, for example, !Xóõ, the African language spoken by a few thousand people in Botswana and Namibia. It has at least eighty-seven consonant sounds (compared to English's twenty-four consonant sounds). And many of these are "click" and "pop" sounds nonexistent in almost all other languages.

Getting the Most Out of Your ESL Classes

To get the most out of your ESL classes, you'll want to take advantage of your professors' expertise and your college's technological tools. You'll also want to find out which of your ESL courses will provide credit and which are transferable. And, as you work your way through each course, make sure you acknowledge your successes.

ESL Professors

Your ESL teachers are your most valuable resource in your quest for English fluency.

The requirements to teach ESL vary from state to state, but all certified ESL professors have special training in teaching the subject. And in community colleges, nearly all faculty who teach ESL have an MA in Teaching English for Speakers of Other Languages (TESOL).

Don't be shy about letting them know when you have some difficulty with the material. If an assignment or an exercise isn't clear to you, don't hesitate to ask for a clearer explanation. Your teachers are there to help and want to help.

Technological Resources

Although your instructors are your most valuable learning resource, other learning tools are at your disposal as well.

ESL students now have access to a marvelous array of electronic resources that can aid the learning process. For example, your college probably has a language lab complete with videos, podcasts, CDs, and DVDs that cover all the aspects of language acquisition. At school or at home you can turn to some of the thousands of Web sites geared to the teaching of English. Why not review your lessons on your iPod while cleaning your house or shopping? Or grab a few minutes for a brushup while eating lunch, or speak along with guided lessons while you drive or cook? All these superb learning tools can be downloaded, often for free. Your human teacher can help direct you to the best of these computer-mediated resources.

USEFUL WEB SITES FOR ESL STUDENTS

http://a4esl.org — This is a great Web site that offers activities, quizzes, and podcasts at all levels of English acquisition to help people who speak any of a number of languages, from Arabic to Tshiluba.

http://www.learn-english-options.com — This site includes listening comprehension activities, tips on taking official English language exams, and resources for learning grammar.

http://www.wordchamp.com — Read articles from the BBC or *Times* Web sites with this Web tool that helps you know the meaning and pronunciation of words instantly with the click of a button.

http://www.eslconnect.com/links.html — This site's list of ESL resources includes over 200 links for everything from games to five-minute English lessons.

http://www.eslgold.com — ESLgold offers a thousand pages of learning materials organized by skill and level and includes audio files.

http://www.esl-lab.com — Randall's ESL Cyber Listening Lab offers many audio files and quizzes to test your comprehension.

Credits

Many community colleges teach advanced ESL courses that provide academic credit. In some cases, these classes will be transferable to four-year schools but only as elective credits—that is, not as credits toward your major. On the other hand, with some exceptions, introductory ESL classes are not credit granting. And not only do colleges differ on the credit-bearing status of ESL classes, but even within a college there may be different rules for different classes. The complexities mount: In most schools, credit and noncredit ESL classes are housed in the English, ESL, or other academic department, but in other schools, both credit and noncredit ESL classes are part of the continuing education program. In still others, noncredit ESL courses are given out of the continuing education area of the school, and the credit-bearing ESL courses are given in an academic department. If all this sounds confusing, it is. So don't expect to solve these credit and transfer mysteries on your own. Talk with the administrators of the ESL program to determine which courses provide credit, which are transferable, and what options are available to you.

DIGGING DEEPER

Many students born and raised in the United States are surprised to be placed in an ESL class. Generally that occurs because these students, having grown up speaking another language at home, may not have the strongest command of English, especially in the area of writing. As academic writing requires familiarity with complex structures and styles that aren't typically used in everyday social interactions, it wouldn't be unusual for you to be placed in an ESL class. So don't freak out about this—just get down to work.

Don't be too disappointed if your ESL class doesn't provide credit toward your degree. Passing your ESL classes is a basic requirement if you're to succeed in all your other credited college classes. Beyond school, mastering English is a necessity for flourishing in your career. Approach these classes as an opportunity to improve your English by learning from excellent teachers, using up-to-date learning resources, and doing this together with wonderful classmates.

Acknowledging Your Own Success

One of the difficulties facing ESL students is the absence of clear signs of progress. Learning a language is not like math, about which one can say, "Yes, I've got it. I now know how to solve this equation." It's therefore helpful to mark your progress by occasionally going back to material you struggled with early on in the course and noting how much easier those assignments now seem to you. Progress may be more subtle, but it's no less genuine than in other subjects. And congratulate yourself each time you achieve a difficult goal.

REMEDIATION

Community colleges often require students to take classes that will prepare them to do college-level work. These classes go by a host of names including basic skills training, developmental education, non-traditional coursework, and the one we'll use here, remedial courses.

Whatever the title, the aim of these classes is to raise the level of students' ability so they can succeed in their college classes.

Every community college in the country offers remedial classes, and most entering students need to take at least one such class.

A student's typical reaction to learning that he or she must take a remedial class is annoyance, even anger. Students coming directly from high school expect the transition to be seamless and assume their high school diploma shows their preparedness for college-level courses. But this isn't necessarily the case. California State University, for example, admits only students with at least a B average in high school, yet a third of even these students require remediation. It's important that you don't see the need to take a remedial class as some sort of negative judgment. It may be that you're simply rusty and need a review, or perhaps you never were really taught this material adequately in high school. Whatever the reason, approach remediation for what it is—a positive opportunity to solidify the skills you'll need to achieve your ultimate goal: excellence in college.

Let's look at some strategies that will help you navigate your way through remedial courses.

Determine if You Need a Remedial Class

The usual way colleges determine that a student needs a remedial class is by administering placement exams. These placement exams have been given to thousands of students—millions in some cases—and though no test is infallible, they've proven to be highly accurate in pinpointing skills students need to strengthen. The areas that most tend to require remediation are reading, writing, and mathematics. Of college freshmen taking remedial courses, 35 percent were enrolled in math, 23 percent in writing, and 20 percent in reading.[3] These are pivotal proficiencies students need to succeed in college courses no matter their major or profession, be it automotive technician, graphics designer, lawyer, or teacher.

Don't be surprised, however, if you need to take departmental placement tests as well. For example, you may need to take a chemistry placement before you can enroll in an environmental science class.

The placement test may alert you to your need to take a remedial class to refresh your chemistry knowledge or mathematical skills.

We want to reiterate one more time: no matter which remedial class your placement scores direct you to take, accept the results as a push to study, not a sign that you won't be able to succeed in college. Placement tests only measure your *current* level of ability in a specific area. In fact, students who take and pass their remedial and gatekeeper classes (initial college-level classes you must pass before enrolling in more advanced courses in your major field) go on to do first-rate work in their other courses and have a substantially higher probability of attaining their degrees than do other students.[4]

Note that many community colleges do not require non-matriculated students or students who are not going for a degree to take remedial classes. Find out your school's policy.

Take Remedial Classes as Soon as Possible

Because remedial classes, if needed, are often prerequisites for many, if not most, credit-bearing classes, you won't have much choice about when to take these classes. But too many students, inadvisably, postpone remedial classes when permitted to do so. This is especially the case with remedial math, as students not majoring in math or science would rather focus on their reading and writing classes and delay dealing with their math requirement. Don't fall into this trap! Putting off your remedial courses until the last semesters might hold back your graduation if you don't pass the classes. Get your remedial classes out of the way in your first semesters so that you'll have more choices later on and save time and money in the bargain.

Credit and Financial Aid for Remedial Classes

Here's the not-so-good news. In most cases, you won't receive credit toward your degree for your remedial classes. And this can pose a problem in states where a student is required to be enrolled for twelve credits to qualify for financial aid. However, most states categorize remedial courses as "equated credits" or another such term. This means that although the credits aren't counted toward your degree for the early part of your college career, they *are* counted toward financial aid. For example, in your first term, you may be required to take three degree credits, and the remainder of your courses can be remedial credits. The next term you might have to take six degree credits, and the remainder can be remedial credits. Therefore, as we emphasized above, not only is it important to take your remedial courses in your first semesters to aid your academic progress, but it's also necessary to take them early to be eligible for financial aid from the college or government. Make sure to learn your state's financial aid policy on remedial classes; the college's financial aid office or registrar can provide you with this information.

The first terms in college are often the most difficult, and remedial classes are demanding. But keep in mind that once you master this material, the sailing gets easier.

Study for Remedial Classes...Regularly and Diligently

As you should with all your classes, set daily, manageable goals. (Later, in Chapter 12, "The ABCs of Getting As," you'll find detailed strategies for studying efficiently in college.) Building up your proficiencies incrementally, piece by piece, is important when you're learning new skills or retooling old ones. Do the exercises as assigned and more. Make this part of your daily routine.

You'll also excel faster by applying what you learn to real-world activities. If you're working on your reading comprehension, say, use the techniques you've studied when reading newspapers and magazines. To improve your writing skills, consider trying out the new lessons in a journal you keep for this purpose. Use your new math skills at the store or when figuring out your budget. This contextual learning will go a long way in helping you absorb and appreciate your remedial classes.

Repeating Remedial Classes

Can you take the remedial class again if you fail? The answer for almost every community college is yes. Can you take them again and again until you pass? Here the answer is more varied, though in most community colleges the answer is again yes—most community colleges allow you to repeat a remedial course until you pass. Other schools allow up to three tries before you strike out. Also, be aware that if you take too many remedial courses (more than thirty hours) your Pell Grant will cease to cover those hours.

But you also need to understand your own limits. If you fail the same course again and again, there's clearly some issue you need to address. Simply retaking the class is not the solution. It's time to speak to the appropriate staff at your school. Find out what tutorial services are available to help you, or consider enlisting some personal, intensive instruction during the intersession to prepare you for the next semester's class. And, finally, if even these steps don't work, have a conversation with a career counselor to determine if you are pursuing a career that truly meshes with your talents as well as your interests.

AND REMEMBER...

We've been stressing here that you should approach ESL and remedial classes as an opportunity, not as a burden. And while your immediate aim is to pass these classes, your true aim should be to master the necessary skill. What's the point of passing an aural English comprehension test if you are really still having difficulty understanding what your professor is saying? What's the benefit of passing a reading class without having learned to read efficiently? What's the good of completing a remedial math class if you are still having trouble calculating credit card fees? Passing or even superior grades are not the ultimate goals of a college education; learning what you need to learn is. By personalizing this challenge—by making it about the success of your life, not the success of your schoolwork—you will, in fact, succeed in school. And this is especially true with regard to your ESL and remedial classes.

To make sure your enrollment in classes goes smoothly, read the college catalogue, become familiar with the rules and requirements of registration, have all your paperwork in order, and learn which courses you need to take to successfully complete a program of study.

Before You Register Read This

WE WANT TO SPARE YOU from a too-common frustration. You think you're ready to register. You've selected your classes and shown up on time on campus for registration or perhaps logged on to the online registration site only to discover you've been blocked from signing up for the semester's classes. The system flags that you haven't supplied a needed document or taken a required placement test. Or maybe you never received placement test results that indicated you must take a remedial course or a prerequisite before you can enroll for the class you want. By the time you finish sorting out all these necessities, the registration period is nearly over, and you have only limited classes to choose from.

You can avoid this disappointment by paying early attention to what will be required of you and by understanding the range of courses you'll need to take to graduate.

PAPERWORK, PAPERWORK, AND MORE PAPERWORK

You may have thought you never wanted to see any more papers after you finished your college application and applied for financial aid. But you are not done with this paperwork. In fact, not only should those documents be in the forefront of your mind as you prepare for your registration, they should be in the forefront of your bag or folder. Plan on bringing them with you to registration. If there's a problem, you don't want to have to come back another day.

Immunization Papers

As we discussed in Chapter 2, "The Application Process in Twenty Documents or Less," immunization is required at every college in the country. Schools do differ, however, on *when* you must produce the necessary documentation. Some require this confirmation as part of your application papers, others won't allow students to register without the necessary records, and still others allow a brief grace period after classes begin before barring students without appropriate paperwork. If your college requires proof of immunization before registration, make sure you have access to it well in advance so that you can bring it with you when you register.

Financial Papers

If you are receiving financial aid, bring this documentation with you to registration as well. If you have any concerns about this, speak with someone from the financial aid office to confirm that your financial status is in order.

If you're participating in a deferred payment plan (see Chapter 3, "Money Matters," for more about these programs), make sure that the requisite paperwork has been filed and that you are actually enrolled in the program. All applications for financial aid or loans to cover the cost of tuition need to be completed in advance as well.

Tuition is charged each semester and must be paid in full at the time of or shortly after registration. To prevent being dropped from your classes, take care of your financial fees well in advance of registration, and bring this documentation with you when you register.

DIGGING DEEPER

Studies show that the level of assistance from the staff at the financial office varies significantly from college to college. Don't be discouraged if you don't get the immediate attention you need. Be persistent. Your college does want to be helpful, and you will find someone to answer your questions. To understand and navigate the financial process, check out the Institute for College Access and Success's report at http://www. ticas.org/files/pub/Green_Lights_Red_Tape.pdf, which has both general information for all students and specific financial information for California students.

Transcripts

If you are transferring from another college, be certain your transcript has been sent to your new college's Office of Admissions. Check to see that it has indeed arrived, and find out which credits and course prerequisites have been transferred. This process can take weeks, so give yourself ample time before registration. International students may need even more time to have their transcripts evaluated.

Students coming from high school should similarly check that their transcripts have been sent. And students with GEDs should confirm that their scores have been submitted in time for registration.

Placement Test Scores

Unless exempted, before registering, entering community college students must take placement tests in reading, writing, and mathematics, and sometimes must take departmental exams as well. The scores on these tests determine whether you can take college-level courses or must take one or more preparatory remedial classes. As we discussed in the previous chapter, these remedial classes count toward your status as an enrolled student and financial aid but not for academic credit toward your degree or certificate.

You will probably have a choice of dates for when to take the placement exams, but be aware that when you do take the test, the result will be your score—you can't quit in the middle of the exam thinking you'll take it on another day.

Take the practice exams your school might provide on its Web site. And remember that, although your scores are likely to be stored in the campus registration system, it's a good idea to have your placement information with you when you register.

Disability Records

Community colleges are committed—and required—to accommodate students with disabilities. If you have a learning disability or suffer from a physical (including hearing and visual), emotional, or psychological condition that might impair your academic success, you can receive necessary assistance. This includes assessment, tutoring, adaptive equipment (such as specialized keyboards or Braille devices), interpreters for the deaf, and special testing arrangements. If you believe your disability requires this support, contact the college's disability office well before the beginning of school.

DIGGING DEEPER

The Americans with Disabilities Act (ADA) of 1990 mandates that institutions of higher education provide equal access to programs and services for students with disabilities. If you are a student with a disability, learn about your rights by visiting the U.S. Department of Education site at http://www.ed.gov/about/offices/list/ocr/docs/auxaids.html.

QUALITY TIME WITH YOUR COLLEGE CATALOGUE

Now that you've dealt with all the required documentation, the next step before registration is to prepare your schedule of classes for the semester. To do this effectively, you'll need to refer to your college catalogue.

The catalogue is an essential road map for your college career. Here you'll discover what your college offers, how you can access all its services and facilities, and the information you need to plan your course of study. Copies of the catalogue are available in the admissions office and on your school's Web site. Because college regulations, requirements, and course offerings constantly change, it's important that you get the most recent edition of the catalogue.

You should read your college catalogue from two perspectives: forest and trees. In the first approach, you'll browse through the entire book. You'll notice that the catalogue contains information about all the important aspects of your college and academic requirements: the application process, financial fees and assistance, registration, academic policies, student services, degree programs, academic departments (including course requirements, course descriptions, requirements for majors, requirements for graduation, faculty), special needs and special programs, the college's facilities, and much more. You won't remember all the details, of course, but you'll know where to look when you need specific information.

The tree perspective calls your attention to the details. Whether you're a new student or a continuing student, you'll want to review the specifics that concern you *now* as you prepare to register. For example, you might want to look up which remedial classes are required for the courses you plan on taking, whom to speak to about financial aid, or how to contact the school's writing center. It's also a good idea to explore the department of your major to learn which courses are required, what electives are offered, and the location and names of the department's chairperson and faculty.

Essential Course Terminology

We noted that the catalogue provides comprehensive information about the college; a comprehensive catalogue includes everything from tidbits about the historical significance of the campus's location to descriptions of extracurricular activities. But as you develop your semester's schedule of classes, it's important you know how to read the catalogue's course descriptions. The following are a few important terms:

- *Prerequisite:* Course that must be completed *before* you're eligible to enroll in a desired course.

- *Corequisite:* Course that must be either completed *before* you're eligible to enroll in a desired course *or* taken at the same time as the desired course.
- *Electives:* Courses you may choose but that are not required to fulfill a program.
- *Restricted electives:* Courses you may choose from a set list.
- *Credit hour:* A credit hour generally represents one hour of faculty-structured learning activity such as a lecture, two hours of a laboratory activity, or three hours of clinical or studio instruction per week for a semester.
- *Credits:* Number of credits to be awarded for the completion of the course. Some preparatory or remedial-level courses do not provide credit toward a degree but are included in tuition and *course load*.
- *Matriculated student:* A student who has met the admissions requirements and is enrolled in a program of study geared toward a degree or certificate. Matriculated students can attend classes full or part time.
- *Course load:* A full-time course load is generally twelve credits or more. If you want to exceed the maximum credits allowed per semester (typically eighteen), you may need to obtain special permission. Note that state scholarships or foreign student visas usually require students to carry a course load of twelve credits or more.

College Hieroglyphics: Deciphering the Course Code

The course description, typically a two- or three-sentence summary of the class, will also include some shorthand or code. Although all colleges do not use the same code, most codes contain similar elements. Consider, for example, this listing: HIS 20 3cr DL preq: HIS 10 or HIS 11.

In this instance, the "HIS" stands for history. This is a three-credit course, as indicated by the "3cr." The "DL" indicates that the class is also offered as a distance learning class. The notation "preq" and the class codes following it mean that the completion of either one of two other history classes is a prerequisite for enrolling in this history class.

WHO WOULD'VE THOUGHT?

Don't try to make sense of course numbers. They're often arbitrary. An introductory chemistry class can be CHM 10, 102, 112, or 122. Generally, colleges reserve specific numbers for different purposes, such as remedial classes, introductory classes, special topics, honors classes, writing-intensive classes, and so on, but often a number is assigned simply because it was never used before. For example, if years ago there had been some chemistry class numbered CHM 11, and that course is no longer offered, that number might be retired forever to avoid confusion.

The Catalogue as Contract

The catalogue is a central repository of information about the college, but you can also view it as a contract of sorts between you and the school. If you follow the specified rules and procedures stated in the catalogue, you can with good reason insist that the school honor what is written there. This might be of importance later if the school implements new rules for completing a major or for graduation. For example, suppose when you began at the school, the single required English literature course was a survey course of world literature, and you took this course in your first or second term. If the college later changes the required English course to a survey in American literature, it cannot now make you take this course as well. The college must honor the requirements set out in the catalogue that was current at the time you enrolled in your program. Note that the school can, however, eliminate a program or major, but it must give enrolled students a reasonable amount of time to finish the program.

DETERMINING YOUR COURSES

You open up the catalogue, turn to the section on course work, and are hit with page after page of course offerings. Some courses you dismiss immediately as being of no interest to you. A few are right up your alley, and you can't wait to enroll in them. Still others look appealing, but you wonder if you can spare the time for them. And many seem utterly mysterious—you have no idea what they're about. In other words, you feel overwhelmed by all the possibilities.

And even before you get to the course descriptions, you notice that entire sections of the catalogue are devoted to listing the various programs of study. *A program of study establishes an approved pattern of course work.* Many schools offer students a "pattern sheet"—a recommended order of courses—that can be a crucial guide for you. With this in hand, you're less likely to be overwhelmed by the abundance of courses from which to choose and can systematically plot out which classes to take in the first term, second, and so on. See if your major has a pattern sheet, or ask an advisor for one. It will be of enormous use throughout your college career.

Your program will be made up of courses that fall into a number of specific categories. Let's review these.

Freshman Experience

Many colleges require that you take some sort of freshman experience program or orientation course. Depending on your school, this course can run a full semester or just a couple of weeks. Some colleges grant a few credits for this course; others give none at all. The goal of many of these courses is to introduce you to the school; improve your study skills; help you pick a major or decide on a career path; and prepare you to navigate registration, financial aid requirements, academic life, and so on. These introductory courses go by a variety of names, such as College Success, First Year Experience, and Freshman Seminar.

Many schools, however, offer more comprehensive freshman programs that feature block programming or learning communities. Block programming means that three or four courses are scheduled for you, and enrolled students stay together as a unit for all these classes. So your school may offer a freshman orientation course along with two or three academic courses, such as an English course and a remedial math class. Learning communities often offer the same type of block program along with extracurricular trips and activities. If this type of program is offered, do consider it seriously. Studies have repeatedly shown that students who've participated in these programs have a better success rate than those who did not.[1] These programs are an excellent opportunity to join a community of equally committed learners and develop both study groups and enduring friendships.

Demystifying Core, Gen Ed, and Distribution Requirements

Don't be dismayed if you're confused about the terms "core courses," "general education," or "distribution requirements." The meaning of these terms varies not only from community college to community college and from community college to four-year college, but even from one program of study to the next within the same school. Let's help you sort this out.

Core courses generally refer to those courses that everyone must take at the college to receive a degree. They may include only one or two courses, such as an English composition or a communications class plus perhaps a math class. Many schools do not have any core courses; instead they designate a program of skills mastery or courses that are part of the school's general education program.

DIGGING DEEPER

Students who have completed Liberal Arts and Sciences AA degrees will usually have met the requirements of the general education distribution of four-year colleges. However, because of the specialized nature of the AAS degree, while all their credits might transfer, students with this degree may not meet the general education requirements at a four-year school.

General education usually refers to a program of study in the arts and sciences that provides students with a broad educational experience. In four-year colleges, general education programs are typically distribution-based programs requiring students to choose one course from each of six or seven areas, or distributions. For example, within the humanities division, a student may choose between art and music; within the social sciences division, between sociology and psychology. In community colleges, in contrast, your choices are more limited. An outside agency, for example, may stipulate the course work for students enrolled in an AAS program related to the agency's field, and, as a result, students have fewer course options outside their major.

Many community colleges, therefore, focus instead on general education competencies or proficiencies. These competencies are acquired over a sequence of classes throughout your program rather than in a particular series of areas.

Recognize that courses outside your area of interest aren't annoying barriers for you to rush through. These classes are important to your education. And recognize, too, that students often change their major when they stumble across a required subject that they enjoy. A student planning on a career in education falls in love with the lab work in her biology class and decides to go into research. A nursing student protests loudly about having to take a geography class but then develops an abiding interest in demographics. You, too, might surprise yourself.

FROM THE AUTHORS' FILES

Some years ago, I had a student who thought she wanted to be a nurse. Her parents wanted her to be a nurse; her extended family told her that she should be a nurse. However, when she began her course work, she was required to take a core course in public speaking, which I taught. At her first speech, she rose from her seat, walked majestically to the lectern, and delivered an almost perfect presentation. And every speech after that was equally good. She absolutely loved public speaking, and by the end of the term, she had decided she wanted to become a lawyer and prosecute cases in court. Six years later, I received an invitation to attend her graduation from New York University School of Law. When I went up to congratulate her, she hugged me and whispered, "Thank God I took your class early in my course work. I never really could bear the sight of blood." So keep your mind and heart open when you take required courses. You never know when they may be the start of a wonderful, different, unexpected journey. *DG*

In any case, the broader learning you receive as a result of a general education program will prove valuable in your career no matter which field you choose to pursue.

FOCUS OF PROFICIENCY-BASED GENERAL EDUCATION PROGRAMS

Reading: the ability to analyze and interpret at a college level, books, articles, and documents, both of a general nature and within the student's own discipline.

Writing: the ability to write clear, grammatical, and coherent prose for different purposes and audiences. Students also must master the skill of choosing, developing, and organizing topics and supporting material.

Speaking and listening: competence in communicating orally in clear, coherent, and persuasive language appropriate to different occasions. Proficiency in analyzing and interpreting various forms of spoken communication.

Critical thinking: acquiring qualitative and quantitative skills to evaluate critically arguments and claims. Problem solving is an application of critical thinking.

Computer literacy: the ability to use computer-based technology in communicating, solving problems, and acquiring information.

Courses for Your Major

As a college student, you'll eventually concentrate on one field of study—your major (sometimes called your curricula). When registering, you'll need to be aware of which courses are required in your major and which are prerequisites for these classes.

Many students enter community college knowing exactly what they want to study. But you might not be among them. After all, this is a new beginning, and you might want to remain open to discovering talents you never knew you had. Perhaps there's a natural actor lurking within or a keen business executive ready to emerge. Before committing yourself to a major, perhaps you want to explore subjects about which you know little or nothing—from art to zoology.

Although this is certainly a reasonable approach to your studies, your college—and financial aid sources—may require that you enter school with a determined major. They don't want you wasting time and money on courses you don't need. This does not mean you must have a specific field in mind. You can, for example, choose to enroll in an AA program in Liberal Arts and Sciences that allows you to explore a broad range of disciplines from literature to the social sciences to the life sciences.

DIGGING DEEPER

Be aware that if you major in a very specialized area, such as surgical technology, rather than in a more generalized study, such as liberal arts and sciences, and then decide to switch majors, you might end up with a new set of courses you must complete and, as a result, a delayed graduation. It might make more sense, therefore, to complete your degree and change your educational focus when you transfer to a four-year school. Nonetheless, changing majors even while in community college might be a reasonable price to pay if you find a field that truly ignites your excitement.

Choosing a Major

How should you choose a major? For some students, this is a no-brainer. They've known since childhood what they want to do when they grew up. If you don't have this determined path, answer a few questions about yourself as honestly as you can. Which classes did you enjoy in the past? How did you do in these classes? What sort of books do you read in your spare time? If they are books about politics, perhaps you should major in political science; if you prefer novels, you might consider majoring in English. What sort of television programs do you enjoy? Shows that take place in the hospital? Courtroom dramas? If you gravitate to nature shows, a career in biology might make sense. If you're undecided between two majors, take a class or two in each subject to learn which seems to be the better fit. But recognize that factors other than interest count as well, such as your talent for the subject as well as the practicalities of getting a degree in the field and making an adequate living in the profession.

HELPING YOU CHOOSE YOUR MAJOR

As we've noted, in choosing a major you need to examine the job market and the difficulty (or ease) of getting a degree in the field and mastering the necessary skills. But you also need to determine which field best matches your genuine interests and abilities. Here a few self-reflective questions that call for honest answers.

- In what subjects did you excel? Which did you despise?
- Do you prefer to work alone (as in front of a computer) or seek out group activities?
- Do you prefer clearly defined tasks or work that calls for ongoing innovation?
- Which jobs of the people you know seem most appealing to you?
- Which skills do you have that will help you in a career?
- In what areas did you excel in your recent jobs? What caused problems?

There are Web sites that can help you think through these questions, such as http://www.scholarships.com/How-to-Choose-a-College-Major.aspx and http://www.quintcareers.com/choosing_major.html.

But Your Major Isn't Your Career

Your choice of major isn't necessarily your career choice. You might, for example, major in English but want to be a lawyer; developing your writing skills will certainly benefit your work as an attorney. You might major in math but then apply what you've learned to a career in engineering, astronomy, or computer science. For that matter, you can major in math and go on to law school. Your major will prepare you for a profession, but it doesn't limit you to any one profession.

WHO WOULD'VE THOUGHT?

The federal government has a great Web site that lists majors and the possible jobs and professions for which they prepare you at http://www.usajobs.gov/EI23.asp.

Honors

Community college honors programs have been called "one of the best-kept secrets in higher education today."[2] Honors programs offer qualified students educational challenges that go beyond the usual course work. Not all community colleges offer honors programs, but if yours does and you qualify, this is definitely an option worth investigating.

HOW HONORS COURSES ARE STRUCTURED

Honors programs take different forms. Some community college honors programs provide an "in-course option." In this model, students receive honors credit in a standard class by completing additional requirements such as a research paper or extra lab work. Another popular form of honors program provides independent study or directed reading-and-research courses mentored by a member of the faculty. Still other honors programs design courses specifically for honors students. These classes range from one-credit seminars to sequences of interdisciplinary, theme-based courses that fulfill a general education requirement. Only honors students are eligible for these classes.

QUALIFYING FOR HONORS

How do you qualify for an honors program? The criteria will depend on your college, but in all cases you need to have had superior grades in your high school classes or in the classes you've taken in college. In many schools, this will mean a grade point average (GPA) of B or better. (In Chapter 12, "The ABCs of Getting As," we show you how to calculate your GPA.) Talk to the office responsible for the honors program in your college to determine if you qualify and how you can join.

THE BENEFITS OF AN HONORS PROGRAM

More is expected of you in honors classes than standard classes, and therefore more of your time is expected. So make sure you are willing to undertake this additional commitment before applying. But also recognize the significant benefits of the program.

- You'll stretch yourself intellectually. You'll be studying subjects in greater depth and developing new skills in researching, writing, or lab work.
- You'll often work with some of the best teachers in the school and have the opportunity to develop closer relationships with these faculty members than you would otherwise.
- It'll look great on your resume. Four-year schools and future employers will note that you undertook a more difficult academic path than other students. You'll also have demonstrated your willingness to go beyond the ordinary in order to cultivate your academic skills.
- As an honors student, you're more likely to receive internships, scholarships, and other academic opportunities.

In addition to impressing potential employers and four-year colleges, participation in an honors program reaffirms your seriousness about your education and shows that you're prepared to go the extra mile to get the maximum learning experience.

AND REMEMBER...

The registration process can be complicated and time-consuming. But, as with life in general, you can ease the process by preparing for any problems that might emerge and by having the information you need at your disposal. Think about course work you will need to complete for your major and the best strategy and sequence that will enable you to accomplish your goals. With this groundwork you are ready for a smooth and effective registration session.

Before the first day, make sure your registration is complete, that you know the lay of the land on campus, and that you have prepared the various materials you'll need for your upcoming semester— from parking pass to textbooks.

Registration and Right After—Without Losing Your Mind

ARE YOU CHOMPING AT THE BIT, eager to begin this semester's classes at community college? We hope so. An exciting educational experience awaits you. But you need to attend to some important matters and procedures before you take your seat in the classroom.

REGISTRATION

For starters, you can't begin your classes without registering for them. Sure, it'd be nice if you could simply look through the catalogue, go online, or call the school; tell them which classes you want; and show up the first day of the term. That scenario might work for a few students, but for most, a little guidance and understanding of how this process works will go a long way to helping you achieve academic success. You'll be dealing with the registration process throughout your college career, and we assure you that learning the necessary strategies will put you ahead of the class.

Orientation

Most community colleges offer some sort of orientation for their first-time students. (Don't confuse this orientation session with the semester-long or year-long freshman orientation course or program we discussed in the previous chapter.) You may have received a notice from your college inviting you to an orientation but decided not to bother. Inundated with work and preparation for the beginning of classes, you're convinced you won't learn anything important there and it's simply not worth your time.

But you *should* attend orientation. In fact, rather than waste your time, this brief half-day or day orientation class will, along with much else, show you how to *save* time as a student.

WHO WOULD'VE THOUGHT?

Despite their proven value, a recent study reports that only 38 percent of students attended an on-campus orientation before classes began, and 20 percent said they were not aware of an orientation program. If you don't know when your college holds its orientation session, call the school to find out.[1]

At the orientation session, you're likely to meet with members of the administration, staff, and faculty as well as tour the campus (and visit places you'd probably never discover on your own). You'll learn about the clubs, organizations, and other extracurricular activities that will make your college experience richer than just a series of classes would be. Even your school e-mail account can be activated at orientation—another time-saver. And at orientation you'll meet your fellow students—the wonderful range of classmates with whom you'll be studying during the next few years.

But no less important, the orientation session can help you with your critical first registration. You'll learn with whom to speak if you have academic, financial, or personal problems, again saving you time you'd otherwise spend running from one office to the next. One of the best parts of orientation? An appointment will be arranged for you to meet with an advisor from the counseling, advising, or student development department who will aid you with your first registration. (Some schools have you meet with an advisor and register right there at orientation.)

DIGGING DEEPER

Some community colleges make a distinction between an academic advisor (who may be a professional advisor or a faculty member) and a counselor. The former provides course advice and the latter transfer, career, and personal advice. In some schools, counselors help those undecided about their curriculum, and advisors help those who have already decided.

Meeting with Your Advisor

For your meeting with an advisor, bring any material that might assist the advisor in guiding your program. This includes transcripts, your scores on placement exams (if you have received them), and relevant paperwork such as disabilities documentation. Much of this information should have already been posted electronically, but having it with you can prove extremely useful if the data is inaccessible for some reason or other.

Along with your paperwork, you should also bring your mentalwork—your considered thoughts about your upcoming schedule of classes.

Course Load

Are you planning on going to school full time or part time? If you'll be attending part time, make sure to discuss with your advisor how this will affect your course load. Will you be able to complete your target program as a part-time student? Will your part-time status affect the amount of financial aid you'll receive?

If you're planning to enroll full time, be realistic when deciding how many and what kind of classes you want to take the first term. Some students overload their schedule and register for eighteen or more credits without realizing how much work they've committed themselves to. And don't assume, as do too many entering freshmen, that your load is lighter because you're taking remedial classes. These classes are as demanding as your other college classes. It's a better idea to begin more slowly—twelve to fifteen credits, say—get your feet wet, and find out how well you manage the demands of college classes.

Day, Evening, or Weekend Classes

Are you expecting to attend school during the day? Primarily in the evening? Would you prefer to attend only on the weekend? The largest selection of classes is during the day, but for many who work, this isn't an option. If you'll be taking only evening classes, ask your advisor if the program of study you've selected offers all the classes you need at night, as many advanced courses are only taught during the day. So while you can take a number of your courses on a Saturday or Sunday or even Friday night, in general, unless your college has a "Weekend College," you probably won't be able to complete your program by taking strictly weekend classes. Discuss this situation with your advisor before embarking on your preferred course of study.

DIGGING DEEPER

New York's Rockland Community College, Virginia's John Tyler Community College, and Minnesota's Fond de Luc Tribal and Community College are just three of the nation's community colleges that have made a determined effort to establish and publicize their Weekend Colleges. All three offer the Associate in Arts in Liberal Arts and Sciences, and Rockland Community College and John Tyler Community College also offer an AS in Business Administration. Rockland expands the program even further by offering a Weekend AAS in Paralegal.

Class Schedule

What is the best time of the day for you to be taking classes? Are you sharpest in the early hours of the day? If so, consider registering for a seven or eight o'clock morning class. But if you have a long journey to school or don't really begin to focus until after noon, you're better off enrolling for classes that meet later in the day. Does your interest wane after an hour of class? Then don't take a three-hour class even if you prefer completing the class in one day. And even if you want to bunch all your classes into a few days, weigh the advantages of fewer days at school against the possibility that you'll daydream away the final classes of the school day. Your grades will reflect your lack of attention. In preparing the ideal schedule to present to your advisor, make sure your ideal squares with your reality.

And be forewarned: in the comfort of your home, you might create the dream schedule in which all your preferred classes fit perfectly together only to be rudely awakened at registration by a rather different situation. The classes you desire are already filled, or you aren't required to take the course you thought you were, or, conversely, you do have to take a course you thought wasn't required. When you structure your schedule, make sure to allow for any of these possibilities. Be prepared to make changes and to compromise.

Your Major

While reviewing the college catalogue, you probably investigated which courses are mandatory for your major. Again, the more you know about these requirements, the more productive will be the meeting with your advisor. Depending on your college, in future semesters, rather than discussing your progress with an advisor from the student services or counseling department, you will be advised by a faculty member from the area in which you are majoring. In fact, even if your college doesn't require that you speak with a faculty member in your major's department, make sure that you do so: in addition to reviewing in detail courses and electives, you'll learn much about the field itself.

Don't be disappointed if you're advised not to take courses in your major in your first term. Because some programs, such as the AAS require so many specific courses within the major that must be taken in sequence, you *will* begin these classes in your first semester. However, it's more usual that you'll devote your initial semester to foundational classes such as English, math, social sciences, and life sciences. Thus, if you're in a Paralegal Studies program, you may be expected to take classes in English and sociology before you take any classes directly relating to law. These courses will be essential in preparing you to successfully complete courses in your major in the semesters ahead.

Registration Is a Process

Successful registration involves a series of steps.

Reading the Schedule of Classes

In the previous chapter, we looked at a sample course listing in a college catalogue. In your college's printed or electronic schedule of classes, you'll find additional information about your classes that relates directly to registration. This includes listings of which classes are offered for the coming semester, the hours of different sections offered, where they'll be held, and perhaps the instructor's name. It is important to read this material carefully.

HOW TO READ THE SCHEDULE OF CLASSES

Course number and title ↓		Number of class hours and credits ↓		
PSYCH 10 Introduction to Psychology				3 hrs 3 credits
First-level college psychology	← Course description			
Prereq ENG 01 ← Course you need to have taken and passed				
Coreq ENG 11 ← Course you must take at the same time				
1158		9:00–10:15 AM	T Th	Parker 101
↑ Section number		↑ Time class meets	↑ Days	↑ Bldg. & room #

This is a generalized listing in a schedule—your own college may have a slightly different format.

Registering in Person, on the Phone, or Online: Policies and Strategies

We've mentioned repeatedly that each community college has its own rules and procedures, and that's true when it comes to the method by which you register as well. For example, many schools continue to require that students—especially first-year students—register on campus. But with increased availability of registration methods that use technology, some colleges offer the options of online and phone registration.

If you choose to register online, begin by examining the "open sections." This resource allows you view all the available sections of a course. If a section is open and fits your schedule, you'll be able to register for it. But if it's not open, don't despair. Look for a substitution (if the Saturday section is closed, say, consider taking the available class on Sunday) or perhaps you can reconfigure a workable schedule around the available classes. In any event, accept the fact that you may have to settle for a schedule that is less than perfect.

FROM THE AUTHORS' FILES

I generally don't allow students to enroll into filled classes, since I think the classes are too large as it is. Smaller classes are better learning environments for our students. So when a liberal arts student came in, yelling that it was unfair that a theatre course was closed and demanding it be opened for him, I was not moved to comply with his request. On the other hand, when a paralegal student came to my office and calmly explained why a closed course in business communication was needed for him to graduate and that his late registration was a result of an administration foul-up, his request got my attention. He didn't get the exact course he wanted, but he did get a reasonable substitute, an hour of my time, and my commitment to help him when he files for graduation. The adage "You can catch more flies with honey than vinegar" seems especially good advice to remember during registration. *DG*

When is registration? This, too, differs from college to college. In some schools, the period for online registration is prior to on-campus registration. But even if you've entered your information online, don't assume you've completed your registration without a second look. Have you successfully registered for *each* of the classes you've selected? Enrollment moves quickly, and classes can fill between the time you figured out your schedule and the time you enter your choices online. Have you successfully registered for *all* your classes? The system will accept your registration even if you've actually only registered for nine of the twelve credits you wanted. Have you inadvertently entered overlapping classes (does a course have an additional lab component, say, that overlaps with another of your classes)? The college's computer system is supposed to block such conflicts, but errors occur. Have you misread a course listing and registered for a section of a class that meets at 7:00 A.M. when you intended to register for a class that meets at 7:00 in the evening? Mistakes like this happen all the time. Check again before you sign off from the registration site.

Payment

Once you register, you must pay your tuition and fees. If you don't, sooner or later, you will be barred from attending the classes you've registered for. How soon that happens depends on your college: some allow a month or more from the time of registration, and others expect you to pay up within a day or two from the time of registration. Payment means handing over a check or credit card or demonstrating that your financial aid is in order and your tuition will be covered by your grants. (Having filled out the financial application isn't enough; you need to show actual confirmation of the monetary award.)

Late Registration

If, for whatever reason, you fail to register on time, you can often fall back on late registration. This, however, is not an optimum choice. For one thing, many schools charge an additional fee for late registration. You'll also find yourself with limited choices of courses and difficulty in arranging a satisfactory schedule. In addition, you're bound to be frustrated by the exceedingly long lines that accompany late registration. Consider this as well: students who register late and thus start class late are more likely to drop out of classes, earn lower grades, and take longer to graduate. This is hardly a recommendation for late registration!

If you did register on time but your class has been cancelled, the college will go out of its way and do what it can to provide you with the class you need. But if the fault is your own—you failed to pay your tuition, say—the college is much less likely to ensure that you get the classes you want for the semester.

GETTING THE LAY OF THE LAND

Do you remember your first day in middle school or high school? Can you recall that mix of anxiety and excitement? How you wondered whether you were prepared, whether you'd do well, whether you'd ever feel at home in these new surroundings?

You're older and wiser now, but that same bundle of feelings will reappear on your first day in college. You can, however, reduce the nervousness and avoid the beginner's mistakes by preparing sufficiently for the first day of school. This begins with an early, focused scouting mission to the campus.

Discovering What's Where

You probably know where your community college is located. You perhaps have driven by it or even entered the campus for some event or other. But now, as a student, you need to become acquainted with the campus on a far more intimate level.

Check Out Your Transportation Time

Will you be coming to school from home? Work? By car? Public transportation? On this scouting visit, go to the college by way of the transportation you'll be using during the term. You want to get a sense of how long the trip *really* takes, door to door. Allow for rush hours and traffic delays. And once you figure out how long the trip takes, add at least ten minutes. Everything in life takes longer than we expect. If you'll be driving, visit the various parking options on campus. Finding parking and walking to class can take a substantial amount of time, so factor this into your schedule calculations.

Check Out the Location of Your Classes

Your college may be located in a single building, in several buildings, or over an entire rolling campus. Download a map of your college, or copy the map from the college catalogue. Keep that information with you when you visit the college and on the first days of school.

WHO WOULD'VE THOUGHT?

As are many four-year colleges, many community colleges are now opening satellite locations in unrented buildings—even malls—to be nearer to students who otherwise might have to drive up to an hour to get to school. See if your college has such a site.[2]

Make sure that you know in which buildings your classes are held. If you have a class in one part of campus and another following immediately on the other end of the campus, you must plan for a quick exit as soon as that first class is over. Consider, too, the time it'll take to wait for an elevator or to walk up three flights of stairs. All these minutes add up.

Note that a class may meet in one location on Tuesdays, say, and another location on Thursdays. On your campus visit, confirm the locations of *all* your class meetings.

Tour the Library

The college library is perhaps the most underutilized building on campus. Students who discover the library and make it their second home invariably are among the most successful of all. If you still think of libraries as musty rooms with dusty books on rusty shelves where everyone whispers and sits straight at long tables, you haven't been to a modern college library.

Contemporary college libraries have become full-service information centers. Along with traditional printed books, you'll find arrays of computers providing links to a world of knowledge: Web sites, print journals, and e-journals. People who are not part of the college community would have to pay tens of thousands of dollars for the data-bases and resources that are available to students, faculty, and staff for free. Trained librarians will assist you in your searches and show you how to access these resources from your computer at home.

You'll also find the library one of the best places on campus to study. There are designated study areas with comfortable chairs, an oasis of peace and quiet, and minimal distraction with dictionaries and refer-ence books at your fingertips when you need them.

In addition to being an essential locale for your academic work, the library is also an excellent place to relax. Browse the display of recent editions of many popular magazines and current best sellers. Many college libraries now also let you borrow DVDs and CDs, and you'll want to check these out as well.

Explore the Campus's Nooks and Crannies

Once you know where your classes will be held and have surveyed the library, continue your exploration of the campus. Check out the vari-ous academic buildings, and learn their names—you're likely to have a class in one of these buildings at some point in your college career.

Locate the college learning centers. Visit the study rooms. Drop by the computer labs, and learn what resources are available there. De-termine if child care services are provided by the college and where they are located. Take a walk around the gym. Have a bite to eat at the cafeteria. Have a stroll through the bookstore. And make note of the hours of operation at all these facilities.

In addition to buildings and facilities, you might also walk by some of the various offices you'll be visiting throughout your college years. Stop off at the admissions office, read the signs on the wall, and pick up the recent newsletter. Wander over to the registrar's and the bursar's offices. If you know what you are majoring in, go by that department's offices; you'll be spending a lot of quality time in these rooms. Know-ing where all these offices are housed will save you time later if you need to find them in a hurry.

OTHER ESSENTIALS

Once your registration is in order and you've checked out the campus, you'll begin preparing for your first day of school. There are a few basics you still need to deal with before you take your seat in your first class.

Your Identification Card

Most colleges give you a card with photo identification. You need this card to enter school, various buildings, and school events. Your college identification card is often your library card as well. These cards need to be validated each semester, and each semester there are long lines of students waiting to get their pictures taken or renew their stickers. Find out when is the earliest time to receive your ID, and save yourself lots of time.

Parking Permits

If you are coming to school by car, you will need an important self-adhesive decal—your parking permit. To receive the permit, you'll need to fill out a parking permit form and show to the appropriate office your driver's license, car registration, and insurance. Make sure you call your school in advance to find out exactly what it requires in terms of documentation and forms of payment. You don't want to make two trips, and you don't want to lose out on a permit. Community colleges are commuter schools, and parking facilities are limited, so make sure to deal with your permit as early as possible.

Once you get your parking decal, attach it to your car's window as soon as possible. Decals are small and easily lost, and most colleges do not give a replacement free of charge.

Acquiring Your Books

You want to start your classes off on the right foot. One of the simplest ways to help you achieve this goal is to have your textbooks with you. More complicated, however, is determining the best place to purchase them.

The Bookstore

On your personal exploration of the school or as part of your orientation, you probably paid a visit to the college bookstore. Expect to return there at the start of each semester and during the term as well to freshen up on school supplies. The primary reason for your visits will be to buy textbooks for upcoming classes.

As we discussed in Chapter 3, "Money Matters"—and as you may already have noticed—textbooks are expensive. Very expensive. Texts today include color, illustrations, photos, and other reference features such as page tabs and unusual designs. These bells and whistles are part of the reason the cost of textbooks has gone up so dramatically in recent years.

Many students receive book vouchers that subsidize their book purchases. These vouchers are redeemable only at the college bookstore and are not transferrable to other stores or at online sites. But even if you do not receive a voucher, it would be a mistake to allow the high cost to deter you from buying your textbooks. You will need to own your textbooks and, alas, the most current editions—the ones used in your classes. Effective studying requires that you take notes, write, and underline when you read. You can't do that with a library book.

Head for the bookstore as soon as you are finished registering. Instructors and departments decide on their textbooks months before the beginning of the semester and place their bookstore orders well before the term begins. You want to be sure you get there before the supply runs out. Purchasing your textbooks at the bookstore also ensures that you'll have your books when your classes begin. If you purchase online, you may have to wait weeks before you receive them and, as a result, find yourself seriously behind in your course work.

Purchasing Textbooks Online

If book vouchers are not an option and time constraints are not a consideration, you might consider buying your textbooks online. But first go to your college bookstore and write down the book title and edition that is required for the class, the author's name, and the ISBN (international standard book number) located near the bar code on the back of the book. Also jot down the price.

Now you can shop effectively. Visit several different online book sites to get the best deal. Sites like http://www.cheapesttextbooks.com or http://campusbooks4less.com/index.html will search a number of online and college bookstores for your textbook and present a comparison chart of prices along with shipping and other costs. Generally, you will do better if you bundle—that is, purchase more than one book at a time and save on shipping costs. But make certain that if you do purchase your texts online, you've given yourself sufficient time for those books to arrive.

Consider used books as well, both at your bookstore and online. But be aware that used books often already contain underlining, notes, and highlighting, which may get in the way of your studying. Also, used books may not be the same edition your professor is requiring. So check carefully before purchasing. If you get the wrong edition, you'll end up paying for two books, not one.

WHO WOULD'VE THOUGHT?

If you hate to shell out the money to purchase a book, you can try renting it. At http://www.chegg.com you can search for books that you can rent for a semester, a quarter, or a summer. The cost of renting is often less than half the price of a new textbook. However, although this may sound like a good deal— and in many cases it is—you will be only be able to highlight in it on a limited basis, and it may not come with the materials that accompany a new textbook. Make your decisions accordingly.

E-Textbooks

Recently, some schools have begun to acquire online textbooks. These books are considerably cheaper (since the publisher does not have to print the book), but they will require you to print them out or to access them only online. If your school offers them as part of your student fee, then this route will provide considerable savings. But choose wisely when deciding between purchasing an online copy of the book and a hard copy. Which better fits your needs and will better serve your studying?

WHO WOULD'VE THOUGHT?

Fifty-seven percent of students who never use e-books say it is because they don't know where to find them. Fifty-one percent of students say that when they have a choice, they opt to use an electronic version over a print version of a book "often" or "very often."[3]

One More Visit to Your College Web Site

You've probably been to your college Web site to search for specific answers to specific questions. Now, before the first day of class, take a more leisurely visit. You'll find lots of timely information not available in the print catalogue. Click on the academic link, for example, and scroll through the different departments, particularly the department in which you plan to major. Here you may find brief bios (often with pictures) of the faculty, your future professors. You might also choose to read about the history of the college and explore the various extracurricular activities and clubs (more about those in Chapter 14). You're likely to discover some useful and surprising information.

College Calendar

On your college's Web site sits another important piece of information you should access before the first day of class: the college academic calendar. The calendar informs you when the semester begins and ends as well as dates of holidays, school closures, registration, and events taking place in the next months. This is an indispensable resource that you'll want to visit frequently.

AND REMEMBER . . .

The first semester in college is a pivotal moment in your academic career. It's important to get it right at the start.

There will be hurdles along the way you'll have to overcome. You will need to deal with many policies and procedures such as the rules for registration we've discussed in this chapter. You'll need to familiarize yourself with a new environment quickly and, just as rapidly, ascertain a time and cost-effective way to obtain the materials needed for your classes. But if you allow yourself to be open to this new experience, it will be a rewarding one indeed. Here you'll meet new, interesting people and make lifelong friends. You'll also open yourself to new worlds of ideas and skills. This requires a commitment to hard work. College isn't about getting by and cutting corners but discovering your talents and interests and learning about your world. In the next section of this book, we'll explore how to excel in this learning process.

GET AHEAD

PART TWO

To excel in your courses, you need to get the most out of the syllabus, be aware of the the dynamics of the classroom, and develop a working relationship with your professor.

Classified Intelligence for the Classroom

THE TERM HAS BEGUN. Your classes are in session. You've passed the hurdles of application forms, dealt with financial aid, made it through registration, and completed the mounds of other paperwork. You might think you're home free, on solid ground with little to worry about. All that you face now, you suppose, are your classes, and this isn't an entirely new experience for you: you're familiar with the basic components of a course, the class lecture, and the role of the professor. After all, you've spent years in classrooms: eight years in elementary schools, four years in high school, and, for some of you, even a stint in postsecondary school.

But this familiarity can also be a problem. Too many college students repeat the same classroom behaviors they were accustomed to in high school. The result is less learning and lower grades. You need to approach college classroom management with a new attitude. Even if you've been to college before, it's time to reconsider how to handle your course work, your time in the classroom, and your relationship with your professor. This new approach will enrich your entire college experience and your grade point average as well.

REQUIREMENTS OF THE COURSE

At the first meeting of the class, your professor will hand out a *syllabus*. A syllabus is simply an outline or summary of the course. But its importance can't be overstated.

The syllabus contains vital information: the listing of the requirements of the course, the details that structure the class, and the basic rules. You can think of the syllabus as a commitment between you and your instructor binding both of you to a set of expectations. You'll want to consult your syllabus throughout the term to see if you are on track with the course work.

A syllabus has a number of crucial components.

WHO WOULD'VE THOUGHT?

It's rare for a professor not to hand out a syllabus. But if your teacher doesn't, that too is useful information. It suggests he or she is a bit disorganized. This is not necessarily a fatal flaw, as it might also indicate that he or she is a "free spirit," who will administer the class in that manner. But now you know. And, in fact, it wouldn't be unreasonable if, after a week or two, you asked the professor for a syllabus. For without one, you will be at a loss to know what is expected or how you can achieve that A.

Assignments

The syllabus notes your reading and writing assignments. Many professors provide a specific listing of when each reading, quiz, exam, paper, and group assignment is due.

Calendar

In addition to specifying assignment due dates, the syllabus also lists when class doesn't meet because of a holiday or when it will be held in another location such as the library. Make careful note of this calendar, or you might end up poorly prepared for an assignment or one day find yourself sitting alone in the classroom.

Books and Materials

Your syllabus tells you which textbook will be used in the course, including the specific edition, as well as other suggested readings. (See the previous chapter for information on acquiring your textbook.) You'll also see what other supplies, such as test tubes, calculators, or art supplies, will be needed for the course.

Contact Information

Your syllabus will tell you how to contact your professors. An e-mail address and telephone number might be provided along with the location and time of your professor's office hours. If you receive a syllabus that doesn't include this information, don't hesitate to ask for it. You need to know how to get in touch with your professor when you have questions or concerns.

Grade Determination

Your syllabus should also indicate exactly how your grade will be determined. Will it be based on the final alone? Or a combination of quizzes, midterm, and final exam? Is a paper required? How much weight does each of these elements carry? What happens if you hand in your paper late or not at all? What about missed tests? You need to know the answer to all these questions to succeed in your class. For example, if your professor does not accept late papers, then you know that even if you are ill, you must submit that paper—through e-mail, delivery by a friend, FedEx, or pigeon if necessary. If you're handed a lengthy and exacting syllabus stating in detail how grades are allocated for different exams and assignments, you can bet that's exactly how you will be graded. Late papers and missed tests will probably not be tolerated. If, however, the syllabus does not mention a penalty for a late paper and then you are penalized, you have every right to object to the professor that the penalty was not included in your "contract."

When your instructor reviews the syllabus with the class, take note of what is emphasized. That's likely what counts most in determining your grade.

Rules

The syllabus also lists rules for classroom behavior. Comply with these policies: If electronic devices are prohibited, leave your iPod and cell phone in your bag and turned off. If there's a no-eating rule, make sure to finish that bag of chips before class. (Remember that your teacher's policy on food is always to be followed but has additional importance in a class with computer or lab equipment. A spilled soda on a computer keyboard might end up costing you way more than a can of Diet Coke.)

DIGGING DEEPER

There are many major cultural differences in what is seen as acceptable classroom etiquette. In Taiwan, for example, only the teacher may drink during the class. A student is even assigned per semester to find out the teacher's tea preferences (hot, cold, green, black) and have the tea ready for the professor.

Additional Information

The syllabus may include additional information such as extra credit assignments or the policy on extra credit work as an option. You might also find here a list of helpful outside resources such as writing workshops, small group study groups, or extra laboratory sessions.

DYNAMICS OF THE CLASSROOM

The syllabus and your professor's suggestions give you important clues on how to excel in your class. But to get the most from your courses, you also need to understand the unspoken dynamics of the classroom.

Come to Class Prepared

Seems obvious, doesn't it? Yet, as college professors, we see the following pattern repeated every semester: For the first couple of weeks, nearly all of our students come to class prepared. They've read the assigned chapters, and their homework is complete and submitted on time. They take careful notes during the lectures. But soon the slack sets in. By the middle of the term, most students show up to class unprepared to discuss the day's lecture topic, and only a few have looked at the accompanying reading assignment. This is the period in the semester when the A students distinguish themselves from their classmates. Successful students come to class totally prepared *all term long*. Join the winners.

Benefits

The benefits of ongoing class preparation are significant and immediate. The class hour is so much more engaging when you are familiar with the subject matter. You can tell where the discussion is going and understand the connections between ideas. Having thought about the material beforehand, you know what you don't know, which concepts you're having difficulty with, and which questions need to be asked. You listen better. You participate better. As a result, studying for tests will be far more efficient and less pressured; reviewing information is much easier than learning the material for the first time.

But if Something Does Come Up

Of course, life has a nasty habit of getting in the way of even the best of intentions. So what about those infrequent occasions when you just can't get to your assigned readings before class? You were in bed with a 103-degree fever, or that date you were anticipating went well—very well and very late. For these occasions, learn the art of intelligent skimming. Take at least a few minutes to look over your chapter summaries so that instead of being totally oblivious, you'll at least have an acquaintance with the central topics of the day's discussion.

But if you aren't prepared, do *not* act as though you are.

Few behaviors are as annoying to professors and to the rest of the class as students who broadcast their ignorance of the material under discussion. Don't be one of those students who proudly spew their opinions and ask questions they insist are penetrating but are really only hot air. If you have nothing to say, say nothing.

Location, Location, Location

On the first day of classes, you have to decide where to sit. It does matter. Which, then, are the best seats in the room?

The Front Rules

The answer, almost always, is up front. You can, of course, get an A or an F no matter where you sit, but it's generally a good idea to try to take a seat toward the front of the room.

There are several reasons why this is prime classroom real estate. The most important is also the most obvious: sitting up front forces you to pay attention. You'll have fewer visual distractions in your line of sight, making it easier to concentrate on what your professor is saying. Conversely, you'll also be in your professor's line of sight, which also makes it less likely that you'll do something other than pay attention, such as read, Web surf, talk to your neighbor, or nod off. For this reason, it's especially wise to sit toward the front in your more boring classes when you need all the help you can get to stay awake and involved.

But if you are stuck back in the bleachers, make a special effort to participate in the class discussions. Here's the reality: even in the relatively smaller classes of community college, professors have a (perhaps subconscious) sense that the students in the rear of the room are holding back, separating themselves from the classroom activity. That's why if you're sitting in that last row it's so important to make your presence known.

Think Twice About Sitting with Your Friends

Front or back, resist the temptation to sit with your friends in class, or inevitably, you'll be sharing jokes and gossiping. Listening is an active process, and it takes energy and focus. Playing tic-tac-toe or exchanging notes with your friend may help your social life but not your academic career.

Participate

Do you want those higher grades? Then, wherever you sit, speak up.

According to a recent, comprehensive study, more than two-thirds of community college students ask questions and contribute to class discussions as compared to only a half of students in four-year colleges.[1] The relatively small size of a community college class versus the cavernous lecture hall of some classes at four-year schools is no doubt part of the reason for this greater student participation. Here, your questions, comments, and contributions are especially welcome and appreciated.

Moreover, active participation in the classroom conversation is the best way to make sure you won't fade out during the class session. Furthermore, professors look for confirmation that their students understand and are interested in their class lecture and will note and reward your feedback when it comes to grading.

Are you too shy to speak up? Worried you'll embarrass yourself by saying something that you fear sounds unintelligent? Rest assured your classmates aren't waiting around to judge you. Most are too busy formulating their own brilliant comments to worry about yours. So raise your hand, and have your say, and the discomfort will soon disappear.

Effective participation also demands restraint. Every class seems to have that one student who just won't shut up. This is the student who insists on presenting an endless commentary on whatever topic is discussed, convinced of the brilliance of his or her opinion and convinced, too, that everyone else in the class is just dying to hear it as well. Well, this student's ideas might be provocative, but what it provokes are his or her classmates' anger and their teacher's ire. By all means, do offer your point of view when you think you have something useful to contribute to the class discussion, but do so with some restraint.

Only slightly less annoying than students who pontificate about their opinions are those who insist on discussing at length their personal lives. With the flimsiest connection to the topic as an excuse, they'll go on and on with irrelevant—and often embarrassingly private—anecdotes about their lives. It seems to be of no concern to these talkers that others in the room aren't spending valuable time and money to hear about their mothering skills or travel experiences. The classroom is a shared space, not anyone's personal stage.

On the other hand, don't be timid about asking questions. Good questions can help move a discussion along, as can straightforward requests for clarification. If you've done the readings and have been paying attention, then your confusion is probably shared by others in the room.

CLASSROOM COMMANDMENTS

You won't find these classroom policies posted on the classroom wall, but we've been teaching for a long time and want to pass on to you a few "unofficial" commandments about classroom behavior. Students who violate these cautionary rules do so at their own peril.

Thou shalt not belittle the subject matter.

Too many students don't realize how discourteous they are when they dismiss an entire field of study. How do you think your economics professor feels if you announce with utter confidence that all economics is worthless bull? She's spent her entire professional life working in the field, and now a student has decided that her studies have nothing to do with the real world and she's wasted all the years of study. Or imagine the reaction of your English professor if you proclaim that Hemingway couldn't write or the response of your art history teacher when you declare in class that Picasso was a fake who knew nothing about painting. This student doesn't come off as wise but as arrogant and antagonistic. Professors—like everyone else—are offended when told that what they consider important is nonsense. And you don't want your grade decided by an offended professor.

Let's be clear here: you are entitled to your opinion, and most professors will be happy to hear that opinion. At the same time, a little civility and respect are in order.

Thou shalt not read outside material in the classroom.

It should be obvious that it's rude to read newspapers or books while someone is talking to you. But some students are under the impression that it's acceptable to do schoolwork or prepare for an exam for a different class in front of their professor. It isn't. This just signals that you consider that other subject more important than the one your professor is teaching. And that's not what you want your instructor remembering about you when it's time to decide on your grade.

Thou shalt not turn on electronic devices.

Your professor probably announced this rule the first day of class, and it was probably stated on your syllabus as well. As we'll see later in our discussion of study techniques, learning is significantly impeded when music blares in your headphones or you're text messaging or surfing the net. Moreover, it's disrespectful. Don't delude yourself into believing you aren't being noticed. Your professor can easily notice that your attention is far away from the classroom and will not be pleased. This rule means:

- No cell phone. Shut it off before you get to class. This isn't the time to be in touch with the outside world with text messages. And it's a rare call that can't wait until class is over. In the instance of that unusual emergency—your child is sick, say, and you must respond immediately to the babysitter—leave your phone on vibrate. Don't be the one who disrupts the class with a startling ringtone.
- No Web surfing. If you are permitted to take notes on your computer, do that and no more than that. This means no e-mailing. And no checking out the review of the latest *Family Guy* compilation DVD.
- And definitely no iPod.

Thou shalt not sit behind an empty desk.

Professors regularly look out at students sitting with nothing on their desks—no textbook or notebook. No one has that kind of photographic memory, so why aren't they taking notes? Have a paper and pen in front of you even if all you'll do is doodle.

Thou shalt not have a private conversation in the classroom.

Make the transition from high school to college. Save the yakking for after class.

Thou shalt not shuffle papers and put books away before the end of class.

Class is over when the professor starts shuffling *his or her* papers!

Thou shalt not sleep during class.

If you're that tired, consider switching to a high-protein diet.

DEVELOPING A WORKING RELATIONSHIP WITH YOUR PROFESSOR

Perhaps the most important academic relationship you'll have in college is with your instructors. Developing these connections will not only improve your grades but can truly change your life. Unfortunately, too few students appreciate that most professors are available and eager to help them. Working together with interested, motivated students is the most satisfactory reward of teaching.

FROM THE AUTHORS' FILES

I haven't forgotten the difficult students: the man who told me doing homework violated his rule that he must have twelve hours of sleep per night or the woman who informed the class of every communication problem she had with her mother-in-law. But they are mere wisps in my mind. On the other hand, I truly cherish the memories of Sigrid, who was always questioning, took every class I taught, and went on to become a stage designer; Dennis, whose desire for more and more difficult dramatic monologues to perform kept me in the library for days on end; or Charles, whose questions always caused me to rethink my ideas and who went on to work as a researcher in a medical laboratory. It is these symbiotic relationships—in which sometimes it was difficult to remember who was doing the teaching—that are most etched in my mind. And it is that kind of relationship I urge you to seek. Believe me: your teacher will benefit as much—if not more—than you. *DG*

Understanding Your Professors

To get the most out of your professional relationship with your professor, and thus the course, you need some insight into the professors who teach you. Let's review some essential features for getting the most out this relationship.

The Professor Is the Course

Earlier, we noted how you should refer to the catalogue to get a sense of what your course is about, but it will be your professor who determines what the class will really be like. This is true even in departments where all sections of the same course use the same textbook and cover the same topics. How material is taught is as important as what is taught. Your teacher shapes the scope of the course and decides which subjects are emphasized, what is required, and how your performance will be graded. Intro. to World History 11 taught by Professor I. M. Wright is a different class than Intro. to World History 11 taught by Professor U. R. Wrong.

Part Time Versus Full Time

Many community college instructors teach part time. Adjuncts, as part-timers are called, typically are working on their own advanced degree or have jobs in addition to teaching. At some colleges, an office hour to meet with students is part of their course load. At other schools, it is not, and they may not have the leisure time to hang out on campus. If you want to meet with them—and you should—you will have to arrange a time to do so that works for both of you.

The Choice of Your Teacher Is Not Yours

Community college students don't usually get to choose their teachers. Classes close up quickly, and often you're lucky if you can register for the courses you need—whoever the teacher might be. Limiting your choice still more, faculty schedules may not even yet be established at the time of registration. So shopping among different professors is rarely a luxury you can count on.

Teaching Is Their Strong Suit

But you can expect to have a competent professor in any case. Community college teachers tend to be good at what they do.

Because community colleges are primarily teaching institutions, not research-oriented institutions, the professors who work there are focused on teaching, not producing scholarly work (though many do that as well). This is in contrast to most four-year colleges, particularly elite institutions, where faculty members are judged more for their publication record than their ability to instruct. And, unlike at many four-year schools, your classes will always be taught by your professors, not graduate students working as teaching assistants with little or no teaching experience.

 ### *Smaller Classes Equal Stronger Connections*

One of the advantages of attending community college is the low teacher-to-student ratio. In this smaller, more intimate environment, professors have an opportunity to get to know their students and can more easily notice and respond when a student has a problem with the material.

Of course, this being real life, you're bound to run into a few less-than-sterling teachers as well (we discuss below what to do when you're faced with this situation). But, in general, you can expect that most of your instructors will be dedicated professionals who are passionate about their subject and eager to impart that excitement to you and your classmates.

Etiquette 101

There are rules of etiquette in all human relationships, and there are expectations in the student–teacher relationship as well. Let's examine a few important ones in this context.

How Do You Address Your College Teacher?

Students often wonder what to call their teachers in college; too many get this wrong. We're personally fond of Your Majesty, but apparently the title is taken. Here are the appropriate alternatives.

Take a look at the syllabus. Does your teacher's name begin with the title Dr.? That means he or she has attained a doctorate—for example, a Ph.D. (Doctor of Philosophy), Ed.D. (Doctor of Education), or M.D. (Doctor of Medicine). Most people don't get offended if you don't call them doctor, but some professors take their title very seriously, especially newly minted Ph.D.s, so when appropriate, use that title. If unsure, the safest title is Professor—both instructors with doctorates and those without them are fine with this.

Should you ever call your professors by their first names? The short answer is no. The longer answer is absolutely no. If you don't want to mark yourself as presumptuous and ill-mannered, don't call your professors by their first names without their permission, even if they are ten years younger than you are. And even if your teacher says it's okay, it's not a good idea to accept the invitation. (If you remain friendly after the term's conclusion, that's a different matter.)

And a word about spelling. Is your teacher's name Dr. Symanupopulous? Spell it accurately. Check your spelling on every exam and paper you hand in. People expect others to make the effort to spell their name correctly and teachers expect this of their students as well.

Meet with Your Professor

It's astounding (and somewhat depressing!) how many students go through their college years without once stopping by to speak to their professors in their offices. They've missed out on one of the most valuable learning opportunities available to them. Effective use of office hours will help both your learning and your grades.

WHO WOULD'VE THOUGHT?

Only 15 percent of students say they discussed ideas with their instructors outside the classroom often or very often, and nearly half (47 percent) say they never had such a conversation.[2]

Let's be clear about one thing at the outset. Office hours aren't donated by your professors. Being available to students during these assigned hours is part of their job requirement. And, as we noted earlier, if your professors have no set "hour," they will make themselves available to meet with you at a mutually convenient time. You aren't imposing.

But you are imposing if you think of your professor as your private tutor. Your teacher is there to help, but the primary responsibility is your own. Don't stop by to complain, "I can't think of anything to write about," or, "I don't understand anything we're doing in class." This doesn't offer much to promote useful conversation. Come to the office hour prepared with specific, focused questions about the class material or an upcoming assignment. And if a reading or class discussion has kindled your interest in a topic, by all means stop by to explore it further; these conversations are always gratifying for both professors and students. But don't wait until the end of the term to make an appointment. The time to meet the professor is the moment you get the first bad grade, when you realize you don't understand the course material or what the professor expects from you, or when you're excited by the subject and seek guidance for further study.

WHAT *NOT* TO SAY TO YOUR PROFESSOR

This is a chapter about student–professor relationships, and, as we are professors, here's our opportunity to note some problems in this relationship as seen from our side of the desk. We're sure you wouldn't voice any of these questions or comments, but it's always good to be reminded of what might jeopardize your grades.

- "I missed class. Did we do anything important?" When students ask this question, professors are tempted to answer, "Nah, we just sat in the room and played Sudoku and drew pictures on the board." Yes, missing class means missing important discussion. Do talk to other students to learn what was covered on the day of your absence.
- "This subject is boring. And it has no relevance to life." As we noted above, when students make remarks like this to their instructors, they demonstrate a narrowness of thought in addition to being discourteous.
- "Do you mind if I miss class next week?" Of course your professor minds. Professors take their classes seriously and hope you do, too. Sure, there are times when a student needs to miss class—emergencies happen—and you should inform your teacher when you can't show up. But don't expect him or her to act as if it doesn't matter.
- "I'm an A student, so I don't know why I'm doing so badly in your class." That is, professor, it must be your fault. Well, other, probable explanations for your poor grades trace to your failings, not your teacher's. If you're having difficulties with the course work, arrange to talk to your professor outside of the classroom, and together you can figure out how to solve the problem.
- "I need at least a B in this class." Then work for it.

Professors in your major in particular will share with you valuable insights into the subject matter of your class and also provide you with important information about your curriculum, graduate school, career, and lots more. But you won't get any of this useful advice unless you make the first step by visiting their offices.

Should You E-Mail Your Professor?

Look at the syllabus to see whether your teacher's e-mail address is listed. Even if it isn't, most colleges will list your professor's e-mail address in the online campus directory. Find out from your professor if that is his or her preferred method of communication.

Even if your professor welcomes e-mail, you will want to e-mail him or her thoughtfully. Don't e-mail your professor with trivial questions about the school's holidays or with the trials and tribulations of your research. And don't expect an answer within ten minutes. Be respectful of your professor's time and private life.

The Difficult Professor

As we noted, most community college teachers are good, and some are outstanding. But don't be surprised if you run into a few clunkers. When you're stuck with a poor teacher, your school life becomes more difficult. Difficult, but not impossible. This only means you have to step up a bit. If the instructor doesn't explain the material well, you will have to ask more questions, study harder, and get help from classmates or a tutor. Usually, if you put in that extra effort, you'll still get that A.

Small Issues

Human interaction, being what it is, means sometimes you simply can't get along with a professor. In these instances, you need to remind yourself that both you and your instructor understand what is required of each other, and if you do your part of the bargain—that is, your schoolwork—you'll be graded accordingly. You don't need to personally like the professor or hang around after class to chat. What you do have to do is study hard and understand the material and rightfully assume you'll get the grades you deserve—whether the professor is your best cheerleader or not.

Serious Problems

What do you do when you are faced with a professor who isn't merely a poor teacher or someone you don't care for, but who violates his or her professional obligations? Fortunately, such teachers are few and far between, but you may, nonetheless, find yourself in this circumstance.

If you have a serious problem with a teacher, your first conversation should be with that teacher. State your concern clearly and respectfully. Often, disagreements are the result of misunderstandings; miscommunication can frequently be resolved with a frank exchange.

But if you've made that attempt, and your complaint hasn't been satisfactorily resolved, arrange to speak with the department chairperson. Make sure, however, to come to that meeting prepared with facts. And stick to the facts; don't exaggerate or make unsubstantiated claims. The chairperson has the interest of both faculty members and students in mind and needs to know all the relevant information to reach a fair solution to the issue. Bring any paperwork that supports your claims. If you think the professor has given you a low grade and you deserve higher, have the papers with you that prove you merit a higher grade. If the professor has said something inappropriate to you, and if someone has witnessed this behavior, bring that witness along with you to substantiate your claim. Don't hesitate to come forward because you worry that your complaint will cause you more problems. The chairperson's aim is to make sure that faculty and students work together in a productive manner, and he or she will take your comments seriously.

Professors as Mentors

One of the rich rewards of the college experience occurs when a student discovers a teacher who becomes his or her mentor. This professor can ignite the spark of learning in you as you've never experienced before and inspire you to develop interests and talents you never knew you had. But, the mentor–student relationship is a two-way relationship. You implicitly commit yourself to follow the guidance offered. And your teacher clearly believes enough in you to invest her time and effort. Recognize that, like all relationships, this one will have its ups and downs, periods of intensity, and periods of neglect. But if you happen on a professor you think is unusually wise and has important things to teach you, step out of the crowd, and make that extra contact. Professors yearn for students like this, and it might as well be you.

AND REMEMBER...

You will succeed in your classes if you make use of your course materials, especially your syllabus, and get the maximum from your time in the classroom. You also want to develop fulfilling relationships with your professors—they are your allies in your quest for academic knowledge. Allow yourself to share their passion for learning and you will enrich your own life immeasurably.

To decide whether a distance learning class is right for you, investigate the class requirements, and consider whether you have the necessary technology, time, and psychological resources to make this a wise choice.

Going the Distance with Distance Learning Classes

YOU'VE PROBABLY HEARD OF ONLINE CLASSES, sometimes called distance learning. Three and a half million college students are now enrolled in an online course, and many more will do the same in the years ahead.[1]

Where do most of these people take these classes? You guessed it— in community colleges! Community colleges enroll more students on-line than do all other institutions combined. In seeking to accommodate the needs of their students, community colleges continue to be pioneers in the development of online courses for college students.

Why the surge of interest in online classes? Flexibility is the main reason. These classes allow students to do their schoolwork when they can. And for students in community college, most of whom work, the opportunity to shape their schedules is especially appreciated.

At-home classes have additional appeals as well. For example, transportation to and from school, which can be a considerable expense, isn't necessary. And the dramatic improvement in computer capacity and data transmission in recent years allows for richer, more dynamic classes than ever before. In this chapter, we'll explore what exactly you need to succeed in these courses (with regard to both technology and your participation) and how to determine if a distance learning class is right for you.

DIGGING DEEPER

Community colleges aren't just offering a few courses online; they're offering entire programs. Sixty-four percent of institutions reported offering at least one online degree—that is, at least 70 percent of the courses for the degree may be completed online. What does your school offer?[2]

But before we delve into the requirements, we need to understand what distance learning *is*. *Distance learning* refers to classes or programs of study that are conducted online—in a virtual, rather than an actual, classroom.

Distance learning classes are structured in a number of ways.

- *Synchronous* distance learning classes expect students to be online at the same time for every class meeting. These classes basically mirror "traditional" classes except that you can meet from the comfort of your home.
- In *asynchronous* distance learning classes, the professor and student interact in different places and during different times. Students enrolled in asynchronous courses are able to complete their work whenever they please.
- *Hybrid,* or *blended,* distance learning courses are a combination classroom/Internet course. You meet in a classroom once or twice a week at a regularly scheduled time and place; the rest of your time is spent online. Both parts of the course—classroom attendance and online work—are required.

REQUIREMENTS OF DISTANCE LEARNING CLASSES

Distance learning classes require a significant commitment from you along with crucial technological capabilities. Let's have a look first at some of the things you will need to do to succeed in a distance learning class.

Behavioral Requirements

A commonplace misperception about distance learning is that because classes are held in large part online, they are much easier than the same course given in a place on campus. Not so. Distance learning classes cover the same course materials and objectives as the equivalent course on campus and will usually demand as much time and effort to complete. Convenient? Yes. Easier? No.

Being There

To do well in an online class, you need to show up regularly just as you would in your other classes. There's a good chance your distance learning class will be a hybrid and include some mandatory "live" participation in a classroom. But if it is synchronous, in most cases, you still will have to log on to your computer during a set time at least once a week. Even asynchronous classes often have lectures or "live chats" that require your presence.

In general, setting up a regular time to be at your computer is important. As with traditional classes, schedule specific days and hours at your computer for your online class. If you wait until you have free time or until you feel inspired or for conditions to be ideal, you'll find yourself weeks behind your class and struggling to catch up. Mark computer attendance periods on your calendar, and show up.

It's also a good idea to create your own personal calendar for the semester that flags assignment due dates, test dates, discussion group schedules, and so on. Figure out how much time these assignments will take and what you can reasonably accomplish in an hour or two. Plan long-term, medium, and short-term goals. And meet them.

Interaction with Your Professor and Online Classmates

Online courses aren't isolated learning experiences. Their success depends on your ongoing contact with your professors and fellow classmates.

Get in touch with your instructor at the beginning of the semester. If the syllabus doesn't mention office hours, ask about them. In addition to visits with your teacher on campus, you often can arrange an online "office hour."

It's also important that you stay in touch regularly with your online classmates. You don't have the option of hiding in the back of the room as you might in an on-site class; to succeed online, you need to take an active role in your education. An "active role" includes communicating regularly with others in the class. This might involve discussions in chat rooms or participation in collaborative group projects. Your online class might also establish a discussion board where you're expected to contribute and sometimes lead.

FROM THE AUTHORS' FILES

Larisa was one of the quiet students in my class. She rarely spoke up or participated in class discussion. She enrolled for another course I taught—this one a distance learning class. And now, behold, her "voice" became ever present. She was the most active member of the class, always in the chat room, leading discussions, and posting an endless stream of commentary. It seems that, unlike in live classrooms where the loudest voice dominates, in this online exchange, the one who was most prepared and interested in voicing her conclusions and sharing her observations got the most attention. Clearly, while distance learning classes pose hurdles for many, for some students such as Larisa, this medium presents an extraordinary opportunity to have the interaction with other students they'd otherwise be too shy to undertake. *JH*

Attention to the Syllabus

You'll receive a syllabus for your distance learning class in person if your first class meets on campus; otherwise, your syllabus will be available online. Pay it close attention. The syllabus will stipulate the requirements and expectations for the class and contain all the essential information, such as schedules and grading procedures, that you'd find in other syllabi. (See our discussion on the syllabus in the previous chapter.) Although much of your class will be conducted in cyberspace, a textbook and other supplemental print material may be required. (Some instructors place required and suggested class readings online as well.) Take special note of when and where exams will be given.

Technological Requirements

Do you have the necessary technological tools at home to manage an online class? These include the following.

A Capable Computer

If you have an old computer, you may need to think twice about taking an online class. Many current online classes include graphics, video, and other materials that require memory. Although most recent models of computers supply enough memory (active and hard-disk) and multimedia capabilities to meet the requirements of your online course, an older computer might not. Make sure that yours is up to the task.

High-Speed Internet Access

An old-fashioned modem will be too slow for most online classes, which now include graphics, video streaming, chatting, and other content-heavy data. While not always an absolute necessity, it's highly advisable that you have cable, DSL, or another high-speed connection before signing up for an online class.

Compatible Software

You'll need software that's compatible with the course presentations: a current word processing program, a spreadsheet program, PowerPoint, and the like. Your syllabus should inform you of what software will be required.

Online Class Platforms

You also will need software that allows for communication with your online classmates. Many online classes utilize platforms such as Blackboard to facilitate online exchange. Your class might also have its own designated Web site. It's crucial that you understand how to set up your access to and use these communication technologies and how to get help when you have problems using them.

Campus Resources

Community colleges are well aware that online classes are relatively new, and many students and faculty run into unforeseen difficulties. Therefore, at your class orientation, your professor will be sure to discuss where to go for help and to note the resources on your class syllabus.

Many of the platform-related issues can be resolved online by the college's information technology (IT) department. In addition, you'll find excellent support for your personal computer or software issues in other parts of the campus. The library staff might have the solution you seek, and most schools have computer labs and learning centers that you can also contact for assistance. (And there's usually at least one computer whiz in your online class who can answer your questions!)

WHO WOULD'VE THOUGHT?

Do you think online classes will render on-campus classes obsolete? Perhaps. But consider that in 1913, Thomas Edison predicted that books would "soon be obsolete in the schools" because of motion pictures.[3]

If you're computer savvy and have ready access to a decent computer, you probably have what's required for an online course. But if you're concerned that you don't have the necessary technology, be sure to contact your department of study beforehand to learn what you'll need for the class. You don't want to spend the first weeks of the semester scrounging to make necessary purchases or waiting for deliveries from computer companies.

Learn the Lingo

Plug-ins? PDF? LAN? Firewall? MPEGs? Zip file? If you aren't yet familiar with the terms associated with computer-mediated communication (human communication via computers), the time to learn them has arrived. You'll see these and related words and phrases throughout the semester. Fortunately, the Web abounds with sites that provide computer glossaries. When a strange term shows up online or in your readings—new ones are constantly entering the vocabulary—you can easily access its meaning by checking it on these online resources. Here are just a few sites that offer technology dictionaries:

- http://www.successdegrees.com/online-learning-courses-glossary-definitions.html
- http://www.sharpened.net/glossary
- http://www.tekmom.com/buzzwords
- http://www.4teachers.org/techalong/glossary
- http://www.maran.com/dictionary

Your questions about online learning will likely be more complicated than finding the definition of technology terms and phrases. You might have problems working with programs, communicating with your classmates, or uploading and downloading your comments. The Web again to the rescue. For example, at http://www.OnlineLearning-Books.com you can learn useful tips and answers to frequently asked questions by reading—or downloading—the free e-book *How To Succeed With Online Learning: Techniques That Work* by Richard Van Ness and Steven McIntosh. Use the Web to find out what you need to learn; after all, you're a distance learning student, and efficient surfing of the Web shouldn't be a problem for you!

IS A DISTANCE LEARNING CLASS FOR YOU?

The attractions of an online course are readily apparent. Who wouldn't want the comfort of taking a class at home in his or her pajamas sipping tea at three in the morning?

But distance learning classes aren't for everyone. Perhaps you're the kind of student who does much better in a learning environment that provides face-to-face contact with an instructor and in-person communication with fellow classmates. Will distractions at home prevent you from carving out the time and space you'll need to get work done? Do you have the self-motivation necessary for an online class?

WHO WOULD'VE THOUGHT?

Consider seriously before enrolling for a distance learning class. According to a recent survey, the average dropout rate for students in on-campus classes was 22 percent; in distance education courses, it was 28 percent.[4]

Self-Discipline

In an online class, no one is standing in front telling you to put away the magazine and concentrate instead on your work. No one will wake you from your delightful daydream. Unlike in the sanctuary of the classroom, here at home you will be assailed by countless temptations: ringing telephones, refrigerators beckoning with food, house chores begging to be completed, children or parents calling for your attention, a couch offering a nap. Don't underestimate the fortitude it will take, day in and day out, to block out the parade of interruptions.

Time Management Is Crucial

In the next chapter, we review techniques for better time management and how important this is for success in college. The ability to organize your time is especially critical if you're taking an online class. Procrastination is a constant challenge in a distance learning class; it's so easy to convince yourself that you'll chime in on that discussion board later...later after dinner...later when the house quiets down...later before you go to sleep...later tomorrow morning.

WHO WOULD'VE THOUGHT?

More than 50 percent of online learning students are married with children.[5] And nearly 60 percent of college distance learners are female.[6]

That's why it's vital that you set aside distinct time periods for your online work. If possible, allocate study hours that best suit your learning style: if you're more alert in the morning, schedule your online work for soon after you arise; if evening's your best time to concentrate, don't plan to study at 5:30 A.M. Because you're your own boss here, you can schedule your own best time for your online study. The main challenge will be to stick to that schedule.

Two Last Issues

Once you have decided that a distance learning class is right for you, you'll probably want to know about two other things.

Credits

The successful completion of a distance learning class earns the same credits as its equivalent on-campus class. It qualifies you for financial aid and counts as credit toward graduation and as a credited course in your major. If the course's credits transfer to a four-year college, the distance learning version should as well. As always with regard to transfer issues, speak to an advisor to confirm the current policy.

Grading

To do well in distance learning classes, it's important you understand fully how your grade will be determined. If you aren't sure, ask your instructor. And pay close attention to due dates. Because you'll be working online, you won't have that aural reminder about deadlines for your assignments. You might be tempted to just skim over the postings on the class Web site. Stay on your toes, and keep in mind that getting your work in on time is your responsibility.

Many classes include online exams that must be taken in person at a testing site on campus. Collaborative projects with online classmates are common features of online classes, and your contribution to discussion boards might be evaluated as well.

AND REMEMBER...

Distance learning is a convenient way to further your education. If you're comfortable using sophisticated technology and have the requisite self-discipline and time-management skills, these courses will prove a rewarding learning experience. But distance learning doesn't meet everyone's needs or suit everyone's approach to learning. Be absolutely honest with yourself in deciding whether these classes make sense for you.

To excel in college, you'll need to manage your schedule carefully. This means you'll have to commit to attending classes, overcome procrastination, and master time-management strategies.

Take a Management Position in Time Management

THIS IS ONE OF THE BUSIEST TIMES of your life. Along with your classes, you're probably juggling obligations to your job and family. Free hours are scarce and a commodity you can't afford to waste. This chapter provides useful tips on how to better organize your time. But we begin by discussing the too-common temptation to gain free minutes by cutting class. In fact, skipping class is time poorly spent. Time control in college begins with meeting your commitments, and the first of these is showing up to your classes.

ATTENDANCE

Look around you the first day of class. You'll notice that all the seats are taken. Your professor calls the roll, and just about every name is answered with a "present." Look around three weeks later: seats are empty, and silence greets many names as they are called.

At the beginning of the term, everyone is full of enthusiasm, raring to go, determined to do his or her work throughout the term. These first weeks, students are conscientious about showing up to class, prepared and eager. And then the slack sets in. You cut a class, then another, and still another.

The Buck Stops Here

Unlike in high school, in college there is no external force that coerces you to show up to class. If you cut a class, no calls will be made or letters sent to your home. No one will call you on the carpet and ask you to account for your whereabouts. You're an adult free to come and go as you will. Who's to tell you otherwise?

It's easy—too easy—to invent an excuse for blowing off a class:

- you have a test in another class later that day
- you're in the middle of an engaging conversation in the cafeteria
- the class is too difficult
- the class is too easy
- you're tired and would rather remain in bed
- you're simply not in the mood for school

There are seven thousand reasons for cutting class. But if you want to get As in your classes, don't give in to any of them. Students who show up regularly to class succeed; those who don't don't.[1]

In many colleges, two- and four-year alike, attendance plays a role in your financial aid. Nonattendance may mean that your federal or state financial aid award will be adjusted lower. Attendance may also be a specific requirement of an individual course or instructor. Miss more classes than permitted, and you'll be barred from the class. You might object to having attendance considered a requirement, and, to tell the truth, college teachers differ on this issue as well—some arguing that, as adults, students should be able to choose whether or not to attend class and face the consequences. But that is a theoretical argument about rights, not a practical one about reality. Our concern here is what you need to do to perform well in your college classes. And excelling in your class entails showing up.

Why Attendance Matters

Many students attend diligently because, having paid the money, they understandably want to get the full value. But there are other, more academically centered reasons to attend as well.

You Have to Be There to Learn

Asking other students what you missed or getting their notes is no substitute for hearing the class lecture and participating in the class discussion. You have to be there to discern which topics the professor emphasized and are likely to be on a test. To learn what your professor considers especially important, you need to hear the inflection of her voice, see her body language, and see what she writes on the board. You can't get this information from another student's notes or even from a tape recording of the class.

Studying Is Easier

There's a world of difference between cramming the night before an exam and reviewing material you've already encountered in the classroom discussion. You'll appreciate already having a familiarity with the material when you begin as opposed to having to learn it for the first time.

Learning Is Cumulative

Attendance is especially crucial in classes in which the learning is cumulative, where each unit builds on the previous one. Obvious examples are classes in math, science, and languages, but many others that don't come immediately to mind fit this description, too, such as public speaking. Missing class invariably leads to a frustrating game of catch-up—a game you don't want to be forced to play.

Professors Notice Your Absences

And they care. Whatever their official positions on attendance requirements, teachers generally interpret your absences as an indication that you don't value them or their classes. Your absences may not mean the difference between an A and a C, but they certainly can make the difference between an A- and a B+. You won't get that break if your professor barely knows who you are. In addition, if you show up regularly and have a legitimate excuse for an absence, your professor is more likely to allow you to take a makeup exam or hand in a paper late. Don't expect the professor to be as accommodating if he hasn't seen you in weeks.

Attendance is a commitment. Other than in times of emergencies, it is in your best interest to attend your classes.

Ensure the Probability, Not the Impossibility, of Your Attendance

Make things easier for yourself. If you are a late riser, try not to register for classes that begin at 8 A.M. If you're exhausted in the evening, avoid enrolling for classes that go past 9 P.M. And be realistic about your schedule. If, like so many community college students, you have small children at home and/or a job, that's already a full plate. So be realistic about how many classes you can handle. And make sure you have backups—babysitters, for example—lined up for those inevitable, unexpected problems that will conflict with your college attendance.

But If You Absolutely Must Miss a Class...

This surely is a possibility—your child is ill, you need to finish a project at work, your car broke down. Whatever the reason, cut class smartly. Look over the syllabus that the professor gave you in the beginning of class, and review the material as best you can on your own. Do what you can to make up the lost class time. Plan ahead, and your absence will have less of an impact on your grade.

On Lateness

Remember that first day of the term we mentioned at the beginning of the chapter? Not only were all the registered students in attendance, they were there on time. Weeks later, when you looked around the room, you probably noticed not only that more students were missing class, but that more of those who did attend walked in late.

Coming late to class is inconsiderate and especially disruptive in community college where classes are smaller—unlike in many classes in four-year schools, which can number in the hundreds of students, and you can sneak into the rear of the auditorium unobserved. When you enter the room after class has begun, you're conspicuous; you interrupt the flow of the class, and everyone notices.

In the same way that you commit to showing up to class, commit to showing up on time. Students who show up regularly to class on time succeed; those who regularly miss class or show up late do poorly.

Cutting class or coming late doesn't save you time. It costs time—the extra time you'll need to make up what you missed. Diligence about attendance and promptness are part of the broader topic of time control. And of this you can be certain: you cannot succeed in college without mastering time management.

Time management is not about self-sacrifice or denying yourself freedom. On the contrary, it's about scheduling your day so you have *more* time, not less, to do what you enjoy. Time management doesn't close your options but opens them up. Let's have a look, then, at several key features of successful time management and begin by investigating the major obstacle to successful time management: procrastination.

OVERCOMING PROCRASTINATION

We begin by confronting the single greatest threat to using time efficiently: procrastination. We might make light of our habit of putting things off, but the consequences are serious. Putting off tax filing, for example, costs Americans a cumulative $400 million a year, because once we start rushing, we make mistakes.[2] Delaying routine medical tests results in dangerously late detection of otherwise treatable illnesses.[3]

WHO WOULD'VE THOUGHT?

In a survey conducted by the Procrastination Research Group at Carleton University, 46 percent of people said that procrastination had a significant negative impact on their happiness, and 18 percent said the negative impact was extreme. College students tend to be among the major procrastinators; an estimated 70 percent of American college students exhibit distinct procrastinating behavior.

Identifying Your Procrastinating Ways

If you're a procrastinator, you know the pattern well. You have a paper due for class in a couple of weeks. You tell yourself you'll get to it sooner or later. Why not now? Here come the excuses: you're too tired, or you've got to return a phone call, or there's an episode of *South Park* you simply must watch. You'll get to the paper tomorrow, you promise yourself. But a week goes by, and you still have barely begun the project. You make lame excuses to yourself for why you couldn't do it today, but you will tomorrow. The deadline dawns, and you still have done nothing.

Here are your options: (a) stay up all night and produce something—anything—no matter how awful, or (b) admit that you blew it and accept the consequences.

This is surely not the first time you've put yourself in this situation. And though you swear this will be the last time, you've said that before, too. Unfortunately, unless there's a serious change, it'll be the same old story when the next assignment rolls around.

ARE YOU A PROCRASTINATOR?

Do you have a procrastination problem? If three or more of the following statements apply to you, then perhaps you do.

- I can't recall too many times that I actually completed a task early.
- I sometimes don't get around to returning e-mails or phone calls for days.
- I often miss events such as concerts or sport matches because I don't get around to buying tickets on time.
- I can put a letter in an envelope, and it'll sit there for days before I mail it.
- It takes me considerable time before I respond to an RSVP invitation.
- I typically find myself having to rush to the airport or station to be in time for my flight or train.
- I do my Christmas shopping at the last possible minute.
- I constantly manage to delay before starting work I have to do.
- I'm more likely to first sit down and relax for a while before getting to my work, rather than the other way around.
- "I'll do it tomorrow" is my mantra.

Why You Procrastinate

There are a host of psychological theories to explain why procrastinators sabotage themselves again and again. In fact, a great way to waste time is to check out the hundreds of Web sites that offer tips on how to stop wasting time.

FROM THE AUTHORS' FILES

Some years ago I wrote a book about work and wanted to include a chapter about procrastination. Being a good academic, I was determined to read everything relevant to the subject. I kept at this research, week after week, and soon month after month, until the book deadline neared and the chapter on procrastination had to be abandoned. I did learn a few things from this experience, which I pass on to my students. One is that if you have a tendency to procrastinate, don't rely on your own self-will, but get external help. This can be something like putting money away (for charity, say) that you cannot retrieve if you miss a deadline or putting a friend in charge of your schedule to whom you hate to have to explain your lateness. Think of some genuine cost or discomfort as a potential prod to get you to work on schedule. Procrastinators need all the help they can get. *JH*

Let us save you the time and highlight several of the leading theories. Do any of these apply to you?

- Procrastinators fear failure. According to this hypothesis, you put off the work because you fear that you'll produce an inferior piece of work. Nothing less than an A grade is appropriate for you. And when it's too late and you're forced to type out whatever string of sentences you can still manage to produce, that doesn't really reflect your true abilities.
- Procrastinators fear success. This is the flip-side theory. According to this hypothesis, it's not failure you fear but success. You

worry that your work will be too good, and from now on you'll have to meet this high standard of superior-level work, which you don't think you can maintain. So you hand in nothing or something shoddy, ensuring an inferior grade.

- Procrastinators are thrill seekers. In this view, you're a daredevil who relishes the adrenaline rush that comes with delaying until the last minute; like in those movies, you manage to save the day at the last second, right before the train runs over the heroine or the bomb explodes. The problem, of course, is that procrastinators regularly miscalculate how much time they really need to complete an assignment.

Our focus here is not to change lifelong habits—if only it were that simple—but to meet the more limited goal of completing schoolwork on time. There are strategies that can help, and we'll suggest a few in a moment. But nothing will work without a change in attitude. Procrastination is always a choice. For example, imagine how quickly you'd complete an assignment if you were offered $20,000 to finish it on time or, conversely, were threatened with a bullet to your knee if you didn't finish it by the deadline.

TIPS FOR EFFECTIVE TIME MANAGEMENT

The key to getting your assignments done promptly is to accept that your college work is your responsibility, and the consequences of poor grades will make a significance difference to your future. You can be efficient if you're motivated to be efficient.

With that motivation in place, here are some strategies to help you control your time.

Retro-Engineer

This term refers to the process of working backward from the end. Suppose you have a paper due in a month. Where should you be with the paper five days before that date? Ten days before? Twenty? When should you have your research completed? When should you have the first draft done? The trick here is to be realistic in setting up these goals. Write down your schedule of dates and deadlines, and stick to it. You've heard the old maxim: if you fail to plan, you plan to fail.

But be flexible, too. There will be times when you fall behind schedule. You might have miscalculated how long some part of your project would take, or an unforeseen emergency interrupted your timetable. Don't conclude that now that it's off track, you no longer need to keep to your schedule. Rather, readjust your calendar, and return to your agenda. Stay focused, and your work will be completed in a timely manner every time.

Focus on Bite-Sized Goals

Many college students tend to be ambitious and think they can conquer the world in a day. But the fact is you aren't going to learn an entire semester's worth of Spanish overnight. Nor will you write a first-rate term paper in one sitting. It's important that you don't become overwhelmed with impossible goals. Otherwise, you're just setting yourself up for frustration. Instead, carve out a manageable, doable task for right now: tonight, for example, you'll study the first half of Chapter 3 of your Spanish textbook, or write the draft outline for your assigned paper. You are far less likely to procrastinate when your goal is one you can realistically accomplish.

Bite-sized targeted tasks have the additional advantage of being measurable. Did you or didn't you do the exercises at the end of the unit? Did you or didn't you write that section developing the main point of your paper? There's no fooling yourself about it.

Make a To-Do List

Time-management experts advise list making and for good reasons. In our busy world, it's easy to forget all the many tasks we have to do. And when you are taking several college courses, you can also easily forget what is due in which class when. Keeping a list helps.

When you put your list together, assign a number to each item to rank it in order of priority. This way you know exactly what you need to do first, then second, and you won't have responsibilities nagging at you somewhere in the back of your mind. The Web has a host of free to-do lists of every size and manner. Check out http://www.tadalist.com and http://wipeelist.com, which have simple, easy-to-use lists. The list offered at http://voo2do.com is a bit more complex but allows you to prioritize your tasks. Or you may already be using the Google to-do list. Whichever to-do list you like, you need to use it. Lists, whether electronic or handwritten, aren't helpful unless you refer to them.

One of the nice things about a visual list right there at your side is that when you complete a task, you get to experience the wonderful satisfaction that comes from taking your pen and crossing out that assignment or using your delete key to remove it from the list. Now that's done. It's a terrific feeling.

IDENTIFYING TIME-WASTERS

You can gain effective control of your time only if you recognize how you waste time. Below are some of the more usual activities that cause time to disappear out of people's schedules. Which ones apply to you? How much time do you spend on each per day?

Hanging out with friends	___ hours ___ minutes
Talking on the phone	___ hours ___ minutes
Watching TV	___ hours ___ minutes
Playing computer games	___ hours ___ minutes
E-mailing	___ hours ___ minutes
Daydreaming	___ hours ___ minutes
Listening to music	___ hours ___ minutes
Other people's problems	___ hours ___ minutes
Alcohol or Recreational drugs	___ hours ___ minutes

So which is your worst time-waster?

When You Work, Work

We'll have more to say about this in our chapter on studying, but, in this age of multitasking, it's worth mentioning here as well. You can't study effectively while you're doing seven other things. Rather than save you time, this mix of activities will actually result in less learning and poorer performance on your exams.

Focus is the key to using your time wisely. During that sacred hour you've set aside for your schoolwork, *do nothing else*. Nothing includes e-mailing, Web surfing, talking on the telephone, preparing food, or eating, for that matter. Be brutally honest with yourself; you know your temptations. If you always find yourself Web surfing, shut down your Internet browser. If you feel compelled to answer the phone, shut it off (that's why voice mail was invented). As we'll see, dividing your attention leads to poorer grades. Our emphasis here is on another problem with divided attention—it wastes time.

When you work, really work, so when you play, you can really play.

Make Use of Waiting Time

Waiting is an integral part of our busy lives. Think of all those minutes we spend at the bus stop, the post office, the supermarket, the doctor's and dentist's offices, or the registrar's office. Add all those minutes on hold on the phone or waiting for dinner to be ready. The sum of all these minutes equals many hours worth of waiting time every month of your life. This is time you can put to good use.

Why not use those minutes to study? You probably can't do complex math problems waiting in line at the bank, but you can review the lesson in conjugating one of the Spanish verbs you learned in class yesterday or review the chapter in your textbook you'll be tested on next week. Concentrate on your material by learning to filter out the surrounding sights and sounds. You won't be missing anything you don't already know.

And for those of you who have mastered all the possible uses of the iPod, here's another helpful time tip. Instead of listening only to music, try listening to a lecture on the topic of your courses. A quick search with your browser will turn up a host of podcasts, excellent talks on nearly every subject you study in college. These discussions will give you an additional perspective to the one you're getting in class and in your text. You can listen to these talks while waiting in line, on the bus, and driving to and from school and work. This is a terrific way to make use of those periods of time when you can't do much else.

AND REMEMBER...

They say if you want to get something done, give it to someone who is busy. Busy people are in the business of doing, and they usually can figure out how to do one thing more.

To succeed in school, you need to commit to showing up regularly and on time. And if you have an inclination to procrastinate you need to turn "getting things done" into a habit, a routine way you live your life. Effective time management requires a change in attitude, a transition from making excuses to accepting responsibility. As one successful businessman remarked, "The bad news is time flies. The good news is you're the pilot."

Although sometimes it isn't clear just what constitutes cheating, particularly with regard to plagiarism, committing yourself to honesty is both a smart academic decision as well as a wise, pragmatic choice.

Please Steal These Ideas About Cheating and Plagiarism

COLLEGE STUDENTS CHEAT. And in lots of ways. In fact, cheating has become easier and perhaps more commonplace than ever. But it's still a bad idea.

In this chapter, we look at what constitutes cheating (including plagiarism), how to address the temptations to cheat, what's wrong with cheating, and why it's a really bad idea for *you*.

WHAT COUNTS AS CHEATING?

Cheating is deception. That's the straightforward definition and the one we all recognize. Cheaters in college, like cheaters everywhere else in life, try to deceive themselves into believing that what they're doing is not "technically" deception, but they aren't fooling anyone or themselves. Sure, there are borderline cases such as "borrowing" from a paper you wrote yourself for a different course or collaborating with other students on a project or the debatable case of accessing old exams when the professor is too lazy to invent a new test, but these ambiguous cases aren't the problem. It's the straightforward incidents that are of concern. When you pretend to have mastered material that you haven't or present work or answers as your own when they aren't, you're cheating, plain and simple.

WHO WOULD'VE THOUGHT?

Community college students cheat at about the same rate as students in four-year colleges.[1] Which majors cheat the most? According to recent studies, business students cheat more than students in any other major.[2]

One reason cheating is on the rise in college is technology. In another era, students might carry a crib sheet in their pockets or rely on quick, furtive glances at the answers of the student in the next row. But today, laptops, iPods, and cell phones provide students with high-tech devices to get information from sources other than their own heads.

Plagiarism is perhaps the most striking and widespread form of cheating connected to current technology—and perhaps the most pervasive form of cheating in general. So let's address this pressing issue first.

Plagiarism

There's nothing new, of course, about *plagiarism*—people have always taken other people's words and presented them as their own. What is new is how commonplace this sort of stealing has become. Every week, it seems, some book author or journalist is accused of having copied ideas from someone else. College plagiarism has ballooned as well.

Sometimes, instances of plagiarism are unintentional. Often students believe they've conducted honest research and are bewildered when their professors accuse them of cheating. So let's get clearer about the border between legitimate research and plagiarism.

Know What Constitutes Plagiarism

Let's begin with the easy cases. These days, students can find hundreds of so-called "paper mills" on the Web that offer prewritten papers on thousands of topics. All you have to do is pay your money (though there are free sites, too), download the paper, add your name to it, and submit it to your teacher as your own work.

This is obvious plagiarism. True, when heads of state deliver speeches, they speak words mostly written by their speechwriters, but, as we expect this, there's no dishonesty involved. On the other hand, claiming credit for the brilliant phrases in your term paper when you paid for or stole those words is deceptive and wrong.

This isn't to suggest all your written assignments and papers should emerge fully formed out of your own head. On the contrary, most paper assignments expect you to investigate what others have said on the matter and learn from what you read. But your phrases should be your own, and when the ideas are not your own, their sources should always be clearly acknowledged and noted with accurate and specific references.

College students who plagiarize often don't think they are doing it. There are many Web sites that review what counts and doesn't count as plagiarism and offer quizzes to make sure you understand the crucial distinctions. Two such sites are http://www.indiana.edu/~tedfrick/ plagiarism/item1.html and http://gervaseprograms.georgetown.edu/ honor/system/53500.html.

DIGGING DEEPER

Still aren't sure what counts as plagiarism? Then explore further. Two additional helpful Web sites include http://www. lib.unc.edu/instruct/copyright/plagiarism/recognize.html and http://plagiarism.umf.maine.edu/is_it.html.

Proper Citation

To make clear where you've gotten your information, you need to learn the rules for accurate footnoting and bibliography. Many students arrive in college unfamiliar with the conventions for proper citation, but your professors will expect you to know and employ them correctly.

Fortunately, there are many Web sites that can demonstrate the various acceptable formats for creating footnotes, endnotes, and a bibliography. For example, see http://highered.mcgraw-hill.com/sites/0078612357/ student_view0/unit4/enrichment_activity_4_6.html.

You might also want to check out whether your college has End-Note in its library or computer center. This software program, widely available to faculty and students, makes it nearly painless to manage all your citations in proper form. In addition, Web sites abound that will do all the formatting for you! EasyBib at http://www.easybib.com, the Landmark Project's Citation Machine at http://citationmachine.net, and NoodleBib at http://www.noodletools.com are three of the many sites that provide tools that make it easy to cite correctly. All you need to do is load the salient information in the designated areas, and the Web site will create the citation in proper format.

Plagiarists Get Caught

Here's the harsh reality: if you don't cite appropriately and try to pass off the work as your own, you're more than likely going to get caught.

Plagiarists aren't aware of how many different ways they tip off a teacher that a paper is not their own.

- Bought or borrowed papers usually don't fulfill the precise demands of the assignment.
- The paper's tone and the research don't match the student's past work.
- The source from which the material is lifted is well known to the professor.
- The ideas put forth in the paper are obviously eccentric and unacceptable—obvious to the professor, that is, not the student.
- The teacher has seen the same paper in a previous class.
- The student uses a word or phrase that is employed only by scholars in the field.

And now, in the same way that some students use technology to download papers written by others, professors are using technology to detect cheaters. Plagiarism-checking sites such as http://www.turnitin.com allow teachers to scan submitted papers and compare them to thousands of papers available on the Web. The instructor can then see clearly what and how much of the paper is original and from where plagiarized material has been lifted.

If you aren't sure whether the work you're submitting violates the rules of plagiarism, ask your professor. Why risk an unpleasant mis-understanding?

TEN POINTERS TO HELP YOU PREVENT PLAGIARISM

1. While you do your research, make sure to take careful notes and keep a record of your sources.
2. Document your sources. Whether you're summarizing others' ideas, paraphrasing their words, or quoting directly, cite them. And re-member that information from Web sites needs to be cited as well.
3. Changing three or four words of another's work does not make it your own. Name the source.
4. Cite correctly. Use an acceptable format, such as MLA, APA, or Turabian. A handbook or Web site can help you with appropriate formatting.
5. Ideas you have obtained from interviews, class lectures, or television or radio programs must also be correctly cited.
6. This is supposed to be *your* work. Putting quotation marks at the start of someone else's words and going on for a page may not be plagiarism, but it will constitute an F paper.
7. Even if you do not use another's exact words, using another's ideas without crediting the source is plagiarism.
8. Cramming encourages plagiarism. So don't wait until the night be-fore your paper is due to write it. Give yourself sufficient time, and cite properly.
9. If your professor expects you to work alone, don't collaborate with another student.
10. Don't even think of taking a paper from one of the sites that sells term papers. That's outright cheating, and you risk all the conse-quences that follow if you're caught.

Cheating: Plain and Wrongheaded

Unlike plagiarism, which can sometimes occur due to misunderstand-ing, standard cheating involves no such confusion. Students know when they cheat. What they may not be aware of is how misguided their decision is.

The Repercussions Are Severe

Cheating is widespread in college, but in fact, it is widespread among students long before they get to college. Students who cheated in high school sometimes think cheating in college is just more of the same.

Well, the dishonesty might be the same, but the consequences sure aren't. Get caught cheating in high school, and you'll get into some trouble. You'll perhaps receive an F for the test or a note placed in your file but usually not much worse, especially if you're a first-time offender. Not so in college, where the administrators take this offense very seriously. College students are considered adults and responsible for their choices; the excuses of a high school kid won't cut it.

Almost universally, colleges have adopted codes or statements on academic honesty. These are the ethical standards applied to the academic conduct of all students. You can usually find these spelled out in great detail on the college Web site and in the catalogue. Penalties range from failing the work in question to flunking the course to expulsion from the institution.

If you think this is meant to scare you, it is. Because—all morality considerations and your sense of self-pride aside—getting caught cheating invites very serious repercussions.

Although it's true that professors don't always notice cheating, they do catch it more frequently than students suppose. Often, the teacher prefers not to confront the cheater in front of the entire class but later in private. So although these students think at the time they're getting away with their cheating, they're just not getting reprimanded in front of an audience. Their punishment will come later, in private.

The bottom line here is that, considering the severity of the penalty, cheating is simply not a smart choice.

Confronting the Temptation

The temptations to cheat are powerful in college years. To overcome the urge to cheat, you first need to delineate just what these temptations are.

Let's begin by considering a few of the more appealing excuses for cheating.

Everyone Cheats

This is surely the most common and convincing of all excuses. We can divide the argument into two parts.

The first is a claim about the prevalence of dishonesty in general. The "everyone" here is global and refers to people across the professions: the steady dose of CEOs caught engaged in financial fraud, the politicians we expect to lie, and the countless people we hear are cheating at their jobs or in their private lives. But the old maxim about two wrongs not making a right is true after all. And let's remember, too, that most people go about their business and private lives honestly.

But the second scope of the "everyone cheats" defense is even more alluring to students. This "everyone" refers not to the public at large, but to one's own classmates. According to this argument, if other people in the class are cheating, you put yourself at an unfair disadvantage by not cheating. Therefore—or so goes the excuse—all you're doing by cheating is leveling the playing field.

But the fact is most people in the class do their own work, and *cheating harms the many who do play by the rules.*

FROM THE AUTHORS' FILES

Teach long enough, and you'll witness all sorts of cheating in your classes. I've caught students reading from cheat sheets wrapped around their soda bottles, reading from notes taped to the inside of their caps, sending photos of an answer sheet from their cell phones—all sorts of tricks. But I'd rather not give anyone ideas. These students might think they're being very clever, but that isn't how we see it. I'm much more impressed with students who study and perform well on exams on their own. Professors take cheating personally. After all, we're the target of the deceit and don't take kindly to the disrespect. When a student who has worked hard all semester admits that he or she is unprepared for a test, I might be willing to give that student a break. Never the cheaters. There's never an excuse for a violation of this kind. *JH*

The Work's Too Hard, the Demands Unfair

Some students think they have a right to "help" from outside sources because the course work is too difficult. But the reality of college is that some courses are more difficult than others, and you might not be able to get an A in these classes or even pass them without extra studying. Moreover, the class requirements are the same for everyone, and most accept the challenge without resorting to illegal advantages.

The Professor Is a Jerk

So? Is it okay to steal from a bank because the teller is obnoxious?

I'll Cheat Just This Once

That's what the cheater said the last time. As did the drunk driver and the person who lied on his tax return.

I'll Get Away With It

Sometimes you will. But the chance of getting caught cheating is high. Cheating is similar to other law breaking: you get away with it one time, and you're more likely to do it again and again, and eventually you *will* get caught.

I Have No Choice

There may be times when the temptation to cheat appears to you to be justifiable. Your child was sick or had an asthma attack, so you were unable to study, or you yourself were too sick to gather the energy to do the research and write the paper in your own words. If these are your reasons for not being prepared, explain the situation to your professor. In most cases, your teacher will be willing to make appropriate accommodations for you. But don't expect sympathy later if you just go ahead and cheat and, as is likely, get caught. It's difficult to reestablish credibility once you've been found to be deceitful.

WHY YOU SHOULDN'T CHEAT

The central issue with regard to cheating is *your* integrity, not anyone else's. It doesn't matter that other people violate the principles of fairness; it does matter if you do. Cheating reflects your attitude about your core values.

Ask yourself if you'd be satisfied winning a one-on-one basketball game because your opponent forgot the score. Do you think you'd feel gratified if you beat your competitor in a chess game by swiping his rook when he wasn't looking? Would you be content becoming rich by taking money from someone's pocket or from a bank vault? And think of how you'd react if you discovered that your doctor cheated on his medical exams and was just faking his way through your operation? Is it all right for you to cheat to get good grades but not him?

Genuine satisfaction comes from deserving your success. The As you get the honest way really belong to you, not to the student in the next row or to the company that sells term papers.

We don't mean to sound preachy, but the stakes here are serious. Cheating not only isn't worth the risk, it also is a reflection of how you want to go about living your life. In the long run, cheaters only cheat themselves. So this is one of the promises you ought to make to yourself as you begin your college career: You'll take your integrity seriously. You'll accept whatever grades you get—the good and the bad—but they will be your grades, not someone else's. That's the only way to win in school and life.

AND REMEMBER...

Cheating, always frequent in college, is becoming even more commonplace as students use the increasingly available resources to illegitimately help themselves, particularly to plagiarize. But the excuses don't refute the truth that cheating undermines your learning and your integrity. If the immorality does not deter you, you still shouldn't cheat or plagiarize. If you are caught—and you are likely to be caught—the career, the education, and the life you were planning will be lost.

The game plan for obtaining a high grade point average is straightforward: take studying seriously and master the art of writing essays and papers.

The ABCs of Getting As

HOW ARE YOU DOING IN COLLEGE ACADEMICALLY?

Your advisor will want to know. The schools you apply to will want to know. So will your potential employers. Your uncle and grandmother, too. And so do you. In the following discussions, we'll review strategies for studying effectively and writing superior papers; in the next chapter, we'll offer tips for how to excel on your exams. But before we get to those discussions, let's review the essential tool for measuring the outcomes of these efforts: your grades.

GRADE POINT AVERAGE

The most relied-upon standard for appraising your college work is your grade point average, or GPA.

What Is a GPA?

We want to emphasize at the outset that your GPA is a measure of the grades you received in class—no less but no more. It is *not* a precise reflection of how much you've actually learned. Some students earn their A averages by taking only undemanding classes taught by professors with a reputation for being "easy graders"; on the other hand, some B students have taken more difficult classes without regard to the teacher's grading history and have made enormous intellectual strides. Grades don't necessarily reflect genuine achievement.

Calculating Your GPA

Although grade point averages might not tell you everything, they do tell you a great deal. And because this is the measurement that counts most in assessing your academic achievement, you need to know how to calculate your GPA.

First, let's define the terms that enter the equation.

- *Credit hours* refers to the number of hours assigned to a course. You'll find this number listed in both the semester's schedule of classes and the college catalogue. The hours can range from one hour (for example, some physical education classes) to six hours (for example, science classes with labs).
- *Grade value* refers to the numerical value assigned to a grade. Generally these values are assigned as follows:

  A+ = 4.3 points
  A = 4.0 points
  A- = 3.7 points
  B+ = 3.3 points
  B = 3.0 points
  B- = 2.7 points
  C+ = 2.3 points
  C = 2.0 points
  C- = 1.7 points
  D+ = 1.3 points
  D = 1.0 point
  D- = 0.7 point
  F = 0.0 point

- *Grade point* is the number of credit hours for a course times the grade value. Suppose you took Math 10, a 3-hour class, and earned a B+. Multiplying the semester hours, 3, by the value for the B+ grade, 3.3, gives you 9.9 as the grade point for the course.

Grade point average is calculated by dividing the total amount of grade points earned by the total amount of credit hours attempted.

Grades and grading procedures vary from school to school. In most colleges, you receive credit for a class with a grade of D- or higher; however, some schools require a minimum of a D. Some college classes can be taken pass/fail; a passing grade awards you credit for the course but does not affect your grade point average. Other schools do not offer the pass/fail option. Each college has additional grading procedures for classes from which a student has withdrawn or failed to complete and rules for how many classes a student may attend before withdrawing without receiving a grade. *With all these various grading options, it is imperative that you thoroughly understand your own school's grading system.*

There are three grade point averages you will want to calculate. One is your cumulative GPA, the grade point average for all your terms; the second is your GPA for each semester; and the third is your GPA in your major.

Cumulative Grade Point Average

You will want to keep track of your cumulative grade point average, the average of your grades throughout your college career. It's your cumulative GPA that determines your academic standing, whether you can graduate, and your eligibility for honors or, conversely, whether you will be placed on academic probation. And it's your cumulative GPA that matters to four-year schools when you're seeking to transfer and to your employers when you apply for a job.

Your cumulative GPA is calculated by dividing the total number of grade points you have earned by the total number of relevant credit hours.

Let's take a look at Matt's GPA after three semesters of college. First we determine the total of his grade points for all three semesters and then divide that number by his total credit hours. So if his total grade points for the three semesters equals 105, and he has completed 38 credit hours, his cumulative GPA for the three terms is 2.7 (roughly a B-).

Semester Grade Point Average

By looking at your GPA semester-to-semester, you can judge whether your grades are improving or declining. At registration, your advisor will consider your overall GPA but will also be interested in how well you performed in your most recent term. To calculate a semester grade point average, determine the number of grade points by the method noted above (semester hours × grade value) for each course and add them together. Divide this sum of grade points for the semester by the number of credit hours of courses in that term for which you received a letter grade. That's your GPA for the semester in question.

Here's an example. Matt took four 3-credit courses last term. He received one A-, two Bs, and one C-.

Total credit hours: 4 [courses] × 3 [credit hours each] = **12**
Total grade points: (3 × 3.7 [this is his A-]) + (3 × 3 [one of his Bs])
+ (3 × 3 [his other B]) + (3 × 1.7 [his C-]) = **34.2**
GPA for the semester: 34.2 [total grade points] / 12 [total credit hours] = **2.85**

Your GPA in Your Major

If you'll be looking for a job when you graduate, your GPA in your major will be especially important. For example, you might not have done as well as you'd have liked in required subjects such as history and biology, lowering your GPA as a result, but performed much better in business administration, the subject of your major. In this case, you should focus on your GPA in your major when you write your résumé. (In Chapter 16, "The Real World: Landing the First Job of Your New Career," we discuss in detail résumés and getting your first job.) Compute your major GPA using the same process as you used to compute your cumulative GPA, but only average the courses and grades in your major.

GPA Calculators

The math required to figure out your GPA is really quite simple. But in this era of the Web, it's even easier. Numerous Web sites do the calculations for you; plug in the relevant numbers, and they'll do the rest. One of these helpful sites is Foothill College's GPA Calculator at http://www.foothill.edu/transfer/counseling.calc.html. You can find other useful sites by searching for something like "calculating your GPA in college" using Google's search tool. There's even a Web site that asks you to enter the GPA you'd like to have and then calculates the grades you'll need going forward to achieve that GPA. You can find this calculator at http://www.back2college.com/raisegpa.htm.

Grades Aren't Everything, But They Certainly Matter

In a perfect world, your grades would accurately reflect how well you've performed in your classes. But, as noted, grades never measure with precision how much you've gotten out of a class or even how well you really understood the material. Recognize, too, that grades gauge output, not effort; you won't do well without effort, but like shots in a basketball game, it's the result that gets scored, not the attempt. So if you've tried hard and learned much in your class, consider yourself to have succeeded even if you couldn't translate that knowledge into high grades on your exams. Grades are judgments of your work, not judgments of you.

But this is the real world, where grades do matter for your further education and employment. To be sure, you can graduate with a C average, but barely passing grades aren't good enough for you and shouldn't be. So how do you get the superior grades? Two necessary ingredients are diligent study and competent college writing. Unfortunately, there aren't any shortcuts to meeting either of these requirements, but there are strategies that can help you improve in both arenas. Let's have a look.

EFFECTIVE STUDYING

To get the GPA you want, you need to recognize two essential facts: (1) you won't do well without putting in some serious studying, and (2) you need to reexamine—and perhaps break—old study habits. The first point should be obvious; college classes are demanding, and you can't expect to skate your way through them. The second point, though, deserves closer attention. Studying for exams isn't completely new for you (after all, you did make it to college), and, most likely, when you sit down to review your notes, you go about it much the same way you always did. But the study techniques required in college aren't the same as in high school. Too many college students rely on old, inferior study habits and perform worse than they would were they to adopt better study habits.

The crucial ingredient for improved study habits is honesty. You need to determine what *really* works for you, not what you'd like to work for you. Are you ready?

The Study Environment: Where and When

There is no one best way to learn what applies to everyone. For example, some of us learn best when presented with visual information, with images rather than words, while others retain data better when it's presented audibly, preferring hearing to seeing. Still others are hands-on learners. The same is true of study environments. You might concentrate best in silence, alone in your room, or perhaps in a place like the library, where others around you are studying as well. Or perhaps you do your best work in public spaces, such as Starbucks or a park bench, surrounded by the background noise of people talking. And it's certainly possible that *where* you focus best depends on *what* you're focusing on: the train station might work well for you when you're reading fiction but not when you're reviewing for a chemistry exam.

Here's the crucial point: you need to be utterly truthful about determining where you are most able to concentrate. Don't deceive yourself into believing you study well in the cafeteria with your friends hanging out at the adjoining table (most unlikely). Choosing the right place to study is about eliminating the temptation not to study. Be prepared to put yourself in an environment where you have no access to your cell phone, the Internet, food, family, and friends. Discipline is the name of the game here.

And don't assume you already know where you study best. What was true earlier in your life might have changed. A couple of years ago, you might have managed to do your schoolwork in a busy diner, but now the noise and the smells are impossibly distracting. So experiment. Try out various locations, and go where the results lead you.

What time of day is best to study? This, too, is a matter of individual inclination. Some of us are sharpest early in the morning, others late at night. But be aware that our biorhythms also change as we get older; those just out of high school might find themselves absolutely dragging in the morning but wide awake during those hours as they get older. Schedule your study hours when you are most alert.

The Multitask Delusion

You can't study at your optimum while also doing something else. The research is clear about this: when you try to divide your attention between different tasks, each suffers as a result.[1]

This notion that you can study efficiently while doing something else is perhaps the most pervasive of student self-deceptions. Now, it's probably true that today's college students are more adept at multitasking than ever before. Perhaps you, too, can talk on the phone while toggling between your Facebook profile and a video game, momentarily answering a text message and stealing looks at the television. And of course, all this time you're downloading the latest song from your favorite artist off iTunes. But what you cannot add to this mix is effective learning. Effective learning demands one's *full* attention.

 DIGGING DEEPER

Many of us prefer to have music in the background while we're busy at other tasks. But learning is decidedly impaired when the music contains lyrics and the words are essential to the song. The more you pay attention to the words of a song, the less you can focus on the words you're reading.

Partial attention also results in partial memory. Often the reason we can't recall something is because we weren't paying enough attention to the information when we first received it. When you divide your attention between your schoolwork and some other activity, you're more apt to forget what you learned.[2] When you study, do just that—study.

Study Techniques

There are specific techniques that have been shown to significantly increase the effectiveness of study time.

Set Study Goals

Studying is not about how many minutes you sit with a textbook in front of you. Studying is about real learning—absorbing new information and committing it to memory. The efficient way to accomplish this is to determine what you want to get done for a particular study session—how many pages of the book to read, how many of the problem sets to do, or how many verbs to conjugate. In setting up your task for the study session, don't be too easy on yourself, but be realistic as well. Too little, and you won't accomplish what needs to be accomplished; too much, and you'll be discouraged by not having achieved what you thought you would. Determine the length of your study period by basing it on the amount of material you need to cover, not on the clock.

WHO WOULD'VE THOUGHT?

According to a recent study by market research firm Student Monitor, college women are 35 percent more likely than men to study daily, 21 percent more likely to study fifteen or more hours weekly, and 23 percent more likely to read their textbook thoroughly.[3]

Take Strategic Breaks

There's a limit to how long anyone can maintain concentration. Are your eyes beginning to glaze over as you look at the page? Do you suddenly realize that you've read the same paragraph twice? Perhaps your mind is wandering: Who played the boyfriend in that movie you saw last week? Didn't you promise to make a phone call this morning? Is that your stomach growling from hunger?

It's time for a break. Allow yourself to do this. Studying in short time spurts—twenty- to fifty-minute chunks—is much more effective than in long, marathon study sessions.

Perhaps take a five-minute walk. Do some stretching. Sit still with your eyes shut for a few minutes. But whatever you do, avoid beginning another time-consuming activity like watching television or calling a friend for a chat. That five-minute break will quickly become a half hour or more and make it much more difficult to return to your work.

Furthermore, some learning experts recommend that you don't take your break when you're at a difficult spot in your work, because you'll be less eager to return to your study session. It's better, they say, to pause at a point of interest so you'll hit the ground running when you return to your studies.

How to Read Your Textbook

You might wonder why we need to review something you've done all your school years. But, in fact, most college students aren't aware of how to get the most from their textbooks. Do you begin at the beginning? Open to page 1 and start reading? No. Simply plowing on, one paragraph after another, collecting tidbits of information, wastes time. Reading is most effective when you read with a purpose. What information are you looking for? What are you expected to get out of the material you're reading? Learn to read strategically. Follow these suggestions, and watch your Bs become As.

MASTER THE ART OF SCANNING

You don't drive to a destination without a road map, and, similarly, you need to get the lay of the land before you approach your reading assignment. You need to determine where you're heading and take note of the main attractions along the way. Textbook authors spend much time figuring out how to organize their books and title their chapters, subchapters, and sections within the subchapters. So read the bolded headings in the chapter carefully, and you'll have a sense of the chapter's key points and organization. Look at the chapter's graphs, charts, and illustrations. Note if there is a summary review at the end of the chapter.

READ WITH QUESTIONS IN MIND

One way to read with a purpose is to have a look at the exercises and questions at the end of the chapter. Can you answer them? Probably not; not yet, anyway. But keep these problems in mind, and you'll form the solutions as you read the chapter. This way you become an active, rather than passive, reader.

READ TOPIC SENTENCES AND SUMMARIES WITH HEIGHTENED FOCUS

Good textbook authors tell you at the beginning of each chapter the main points they will cover and then summarize their thesis at the end. So pay special attention to the first and last paragraphs of each chapter as well as the first and last paragraphs of each subsection of the chapter.

COMPLETE THE CHAPTER'S QUESTIONS AND EXERCISES

Even if they aren't assigned as homework, by working on at least a few of the problems posted at the end of the chapter, you'll learn whether you've understood what you've read. These exercises also provide a good idea about what the author thinks are the most important topics in the chapter, and you'll likely receive similar questions on your exam.

TO UNDERLINE OR NOT TO UNDERLINE

Let's point out at the outset that you'll only have this choice if you purchased the textbook—another reason to own your books.

When it comes to underlining, college students have vastly different opinions: some never draw a line in their textbooks, and others underline or highlight nearly every word. Neither approach is best for studying.

Learning researchers have found that a far better way to absorb the material you read in your book is to write notes in the margins of the pages.[4] Write *in your own words* the central point of the paragraph you just read, and then summarize each subsection of the chapter (write longer summaries in your notebook). If you can't explain what you read in your own words, you haven't really understood the information; reread the paragraphs until they're clear enough that you can restate the point clearly in your own language.

If you *are* an underliner, don't begin underlining until you've read the entire paragraph. Then underline the main points and the supporting points, not all the elaboration in between. Holding back from underlining ensures that you read critically, distinguishing what is essential from what is secondary.

CHECK OUT OTHER TEXTBOOKS

Here's another tip few students are aware of. While you will need to concentrate on your own textbook to prepare for class and exams, consider getting a different textbook from which to study as well. For most courses, particularly introductory-level classes, there are several competing textbooks, and you might find a different author's approach and writing style (or illustrations and graphics) easier to follow than those of your own textbook. In any case, this alternative discussion will enhance your learning. Other textbooks also are a great source for quizzes and exercises that can further prepare you for your upcoming exams.

Memorization

Most of your tests will require some memorization. There is a growing field of expertise on how our brains input, store, and retrieve information. The following are a few basic strategies for recall that experts suggest are especially useful when studying for exams.

- Use mnemonic devices to enhance recall. A mnemonic device is anything that helps you remember what you want to remember, be it a list, poem, jingle, series of words, or categorization of bones. To help you memorize a list, say, create a word or phrase that contains the first letter of each item in the list. For example, the mnemonic word HOMES reminds geography students of the Great Lakes—Huron, Ontario, Michigan, Erie, and Superior. Or you may try to create a whole sentence such as "My very elegant mother just served us nine pancakes," which helps astronomy students remember the nine planets in spatial order—Mercury, Venus, Earth, Mars, Jupiter, Saturn, Uranus, Neptune, Pluto.
- Organization is crucial to memory. We think in categories. Try this: Write the months of the year in chronological order. Piece of cake, isn't it? Now write the months in alphabetical order. Not so easy. Did you get all twelve? When you study, categorize the information in a sequence you can picture or itemize. If you need

to remember, for example, the functions of the various organs of the digestive system, you might want to begin with the mouth and track the particle of food as it makes its way to its end. You'll find it easier to memorize the names of Shakespeare's thirty-seven plays if you place them into three groups: comedies, histories, and tragedies.

- Shuffle information. When asked to memorize a list of items, people tend to remember best the first and last things they learn. This phenomenon is known as primacy and recency. So sometimes shuffling the order of the material you are studying and then studying again will help you recall more of the information.
- Repetition results in recall. Drumming facts into your head by repetition sounds tedious. But for many sorts of learning, there's no better way to memorize than plain old drilling.

Cramming for Exams

We wish we could dismiss this topic with a single word: DON'T. Relying on getting your studying done the night before the exam is an awful idea. Pulling all-nighters exhausts both brain and body, and when you're tired, you're less able to perform well. Research shows that when we lack enough sleep, our ability to reason is weakened and our ability to remember is hampered as well.[5] Often you'll do better on the test after a solid night's sleep than by staying up through the night trying to do a term's work in a night.

WHO WOULD'VE THOUGHT?

Sleeping makes you smarter. A review of recent research in *Scientific American* (August 2008) reports that while we are asleep, our brain is busy processing the day's information.[6] Studies clearly indicate that a night of good sleep reinforces memory and makes recall easier the next day. And, as suspected, during sleep we also solve problems that have stumped us during the day. So rather than spend the night cramming for the next day's exam, you're more likely to remember what you read if you sleep on it.

But we're also aware that you live a real life, and there will be those days and nights when cramming is your only option. Perhaps you forgot that the exam was the next day or inadvertently studied the wrong material or spent the week before the exam nursing a sick child. All sorts of emergencies get in the way of the best-made plans.

So on these—hopefully rare—occasions, make sure to at least cram effectively.

- Preview the material you think will be covered on the exam.
- Skim all the chapters for the main points, and then concentrate on learning those essential concepts.
- Be selective. You don't have time in one night to read and digest all the readings and class material from the last number of weeks.
- Restate in your words what you've studied.
- It makes more sense to solidify what you've learned than spending your time scanning new material that you won't have a chance to review.

SELF-TEST: RECOGNIZE YOUR OWN STUDY HABITS AND ATTITUDES

Y__ N__ I usually spend hours cramming the night before an exam.

Y__ N__ If I spend as much time on my social life as I'd like, I won't have enough time left to study; if I study as much as I need to, I won't have time for a social life.

Y__ N__ I usually study with the radio, TV, or iPod turned on.

Y__ N__ I can only sit and study for brief periods of time before becoming tired or distracted.

Y__ N__ I rarely divide up my reading assignment into a specified number of pages each day.

Y__ N__ I never or rarely take notes on what I read in my textbook.

Y__ N__ I wait until right before exams to review my class notes.

Y__ N__ When I get to the end of a chapter, I can't remember what I've just read.

Y__ N__ My studying for tests tends to be haphazard and disorganized.

If you've answered yes to two or more of these questions, you need to reconsider your approach to studying. Adopting the suggestions recommended in this chapter is a start.

Homework Equals Designer Study

Some educator once said that if only we called it home*play* rather than home*work*, students would complete their assignments more willingly. After all, who wants to work at home? Homework does feel like a chore. It felt that way back in the first grade and throughout high school, and now you might find it an unwelcome burden in college. But rather than a hassle, think of homework as designer study created by a master, your professor.

The whole point of homework is to enable you to explore concepts learned in class. And while you may do very well on your own reading and reviewing your class notes and textbook, having a focused activity or project that helps you to revisit and apply these concepts is the best reinforcement of your learning.

In some courses, such as math, homework assignments might involve completing and submitting exercises weekly or even daily. In other classes, homework assignments might focus on one unit in your course and extend over several weeks. In either case, you'll want to get in the habit of completing these assignments and submitting them on time. Unlike when you were in high school, you won't have a parent pestering you to do your homework before you watch television. Nor will your teachers be on your case. In college, doing homework is truly your own responsibility.

If you don't assume that responsibility, you'll face two unhappy outcomes. First, your grades will be lowered. Teachers who assign homework expect it to be completed and will likely devalue your grade if you don't hand in the work or submit it late. But, perhaps even more importantly, college homework assignments are designed to reinforce what you've learned through your readings and in class or to expand what you've learned by applying it to new concepts. Not doing these assignments is a lost learning opportunity.

As with studying in general, how and when you do your homework will affect your productivity.

- Determine the physical setting in which you are most productive doing your homework.
- Set aside a regular period in your schedule for your homework and stick to that schedule.

- Get organized. In your planner, write down what homework needs to be completed when and make sure to stay on schedule.
- Don't allow your homework to pile up. If you do, you'll find yourself rushing to do it all in one shot and producing inferior work.
- If you find yourself having difficulty completing your homework, help is available. The Web presents a host of homework help sites offering assistance for college students for just about every subject. But be careful. While some sites are genuinely useful, many will only waste your time. And as many of these sites cost money, check them out carefully before you sign on to their offer.
- You probably also can find homework assistance on campus. You might find it rewarding, for example, to work with your fellow classmates on your homework assignments (but, of course, in the end, doing your own work). The campus learning centers are another useful resource. And many departments offer free tutoring for students who are having difficulty with their course work. Once you understand the course material, completing the homework assignments are that much easier.

Homework is an important part of the learning experience, and you need to approach it with this positive attitude. Take it seriously, and you'll reap the rewards.

DIGGING DEEPER

Homework isn't busywork; it really does improve learning. In a recent, carefully controlled study, one group of college students was given homework in a math class, and the other group in the same class was not. Those in the class who did the homework performed significantly better on exams than those who didn't.[7]

WRITING EFFECTIVE COLLEGE ESSAYS AND PAPERS

Studying for exams is an absolute necessity for getting As in college. But along with exams, your grades will depend on how well you write. You will often be assigned written projects—both short written assignments and full-scale research papers. Writing well is a challenge for all college students, but like other skills, writing improves with practice.

And help is available if you need it. There's assistance in your college library and writing center, which is staffed by individuals whose job is to assist you. You also can access the numerous Web sites that offer writing help, such as the following three.

http://owl.english.purdue.edu

One of the best academic sites for writing assistance, the Purdue Online Writing Lab shows how to create an effective thesis statement and provides links to many other resources.

http://www.utoronto.ca/writing/advise.html

The Advice on Academic writing page includes great hints from college writing professors on everything from developing coherent paragraphs to using quotations.

http://grammar.ccc.commnet.edu/grammar

The Guide to Grammar and Writing page offers a useful approach to writing from the sentence, paragraph, and essay level. It also includes answers to frequently asked grammar questions.

These resources can help you with many writing concerns such as grammar, proper outlining, sentence formation, and thesis statements. But there are many other issues that need to be considered in writing a superior paper. In what follows, we'll suggest some key strategies. The focus here is on the research paper—the assignment that creates the most dread and anxiety for students—but most of these suggestions apply to shorter writing assignments as well.

Understand What Is Expected and When

Your first task in writing your paper is to be clear about what you are asked to do. If you don't know what's expected, you can't meet expectations. Most professors devote class time to review the paper requirements, so listen carefully. Look for key words in the assignment description such as *define, compare and contrast,* or *analyze.* If you still aren't sure what's expected, make an appointment as soon as possible to see your professor for clarification. That meeting might be the deciding factor that makes the assignment manageable instead of a source of unmitigated distress.

Knowing *when* your assignment is due is as important as knowing *what* is due. Even if the deadline isn't until the last week of the term, the time to begin working on it is immediately. As we noted in the previous chapter, the best method for scheduling your time is to retro-engineer—that is, work backward. How long before the deadline should you have a final draft? An early draft? When should you be finished with the research? Complete a solid outline? Working backwards this way, you'll get to the first weeks of the term and to your initial challenge: *choosing a topic*.

Choosing Your Paper's Topic

Students often spend only fleeting moments choosing a subject for their paper and then, locked in to their choice, struggle all semester trying to write something coherent about the subject. A badly chosen topic will lead to a badly written paper. So devote some careful research and reflection to coming up with your topic.

Preliminary Research

Don't decide on your topic until you've done some preliminary investigation. Is the topic so obscure that you'll have few resources to use in developing your paper? Has it been so widely discussed that you'll find it nearly impossible to say anything new about it? Are the sources you'll need easily accessible? Are they dependable?

Choose a Topic That Interests You

You're going to have to live with this subject for weeks and even months, and if the subject bores you, researching and writing about it will quickly become a dreaded chore. On the other hand, if your topic is a problem you want to solve, a historical event you want to unravel, or an issue that matters to you that you haven't yet explored, your paper will become "personal," and you'll work on it more often, more carefully, and with far better results. Don't pick a topic because you think it sounds easy to write about. *Nothing* is easy to write well about, and if you are uninterested, the work becomes even more difficult.

Formulate a Thesis

A common problem with paper topics is their generality. A topic such as "French literature" is hopelessly broad, and "twentieth-century French literature" hardly narrows the scope. Your paper should aim to answer a clear-cut question—a question you should be able to state in a one- or two-sentence thesis at most. The more precise the thesis, the more well-defined your paper. So "How Proust influenced French novelists of the 1920s and 1930s" is a great improvement over the previous topic. A paper on "The economic climate in Europe and the outbreak of WWI" is far better than "The causes of WWI." When you have a focused thesis, your reading and research will be more focused as well. You now have a much clearer sense about what information is relevant to your argument and what facts, however interesting, are beyond the scope of the paper.

As soon as you have decided on your thesis, run it by your professor. Don't worry if you've seen the professor already for clarification. Your professor will be happy that you are on the right track. Explain what you hope to demonstrate and how you think you'll go about doing that. Prepare for this conversation; the more you plan for this discussion, the more productive your meeting.

Writing Your Paper

Write a First-Rate Outline

If you want to write a quality paper, you need to write a quality outline. Don't delude yourself into thinking you have it all in your head and the paragraphs will follow effortlessly. You need to *see* how the ideas will be organized and how the paper will flow.

The three essential parts of an outline are an *introduction*, a *body*, and a *conclusion*. In the *introduction*, you state a thesis that makes clear what your paper will do (explain, resolve, analyze, and so on). You also note the main points you will be covering in the paper and the importance of your thesis. The *body* represents the bulk of the paper and, correspondingly, the bulk of your outline. Here you set forth the arguments that reinforce your thesis statement. You will need several supporting pieces of evidence for each argument. Remember that a well-rounded, effective presentation includes a serious analysis and refutation of the opposing point of view. In the *conclusion*, you may restate your thesis and summarize your argument.

Be prepared to alter the outline as you make progress with your paper. You may have to move paragraphs and entire sections from one place to another.

This is a very rough sketch of an outline. For more detailed demonstrations of full outlines, visit one of the Web sites on writing we listed previously.

Begin Writing Before You're Ready to Write

Professional writers often say they don't really know a subject until they write about it. Writing crystallizes our thoughts and gives them shape and direction.

Don't fall into the trap of spending the entire semester researching for your paper and then staying up the night before it's due writing it. By beginning the writing process early, you'll give your paper structure, and your reading and research will be more focused as a result. Get over your perfectionism by reminding yourself that the first draft is just an initial effort. You'll find yourself paralyzed if you expect immediate perfection.

WHO WOULD'VE THOUGHT?

Students often find themselves stuck writing the introduction to their paper, wasting precious time agonizing over the best way to begin. Here's a piece of useful advice. Don't write the introduction until you've written the paper. You can't introduce what you don't know. So just sketch something of an introduction if you must, but don't worry about fleshing it out until later. This way, you can get straight to the heart of the assignment immediately and not spin your wheels before you get moving.

Use Your Own Words

We've talked about plagiarism at length in Chapter 11, but it's worth reemphasizing the importance of using your own words when submitting a written assignment. No matter how much research and reading you've undertaken, if your sentences belong to someone else and aren't duly cited, your paper will be unacceptable.

So make sure to keep careful notes of your sources while you're researching. It will be too difficult to remember where you got your information when writing the actual paper. And make sure, too, to cite those sources when you quote or rephrase them in your paper.

Cite Properly

We noted several Web sites in the previous chapter that offer guidance on how to create footnotes, endnotes, and a bibliography, and we also suggested you visit your library or computer center to see which citation software programs are available to you. It's worth the trip.

Cite Web Sites with Caution

Don't trust with certainty anything you read anywhere—and certainly not on the Internet. True, the Web is an incredible resource for information, but people can and do post whatever they like in cyberspace. Misinformation of all sorts finds its way to the Web, so no wonder every week another conspiracy theory takes root. With billions of Internet users worldwide and millions of blogs, misinformation gets repeated so often it's soon taken for fact. Your responsibility as an honest researcher is, as far as possible, to develop criteria for evaluating Web sites. Web sites such as http://www.library.cornell.edu/olinuris/ref/webcrit.html or http://www.lib.berkeley.edu/TeachingLib/Guides/Internet/Evaluate.html can help you to assess the reliability of your sources.

Read and Revise Your Draft

It's a good idea to take a break of minimally a day or two between the time you write a draft of your paper and your rewrite. And then allow time between finishing your last draft and the day you submit it to your professor. You need that distance to get a perspective on what you've written, an overview you can't have when you're dealing with the nuts and bolts—the words, sentences, and paragraphs—of your paper. As you reread your work with fresh eyes, ask yourself whether you've successfully covered the essentials of a paper.

- Have you stated a clear thesis for the paper?
- Have you begun your paragraphs with clear topic sentences?
- Does the order of the paragraphs make sense?
- Have you supported your claims with adequate arguments and evidence?
- Do your transitions between paragraphs and sections help the reader move easily from one point to the next?
- Have you put together a well-thought-out introduction and conclusion that relate to your thesis?

If there's still work to do, you now have the time to revise and fix those problems.

Proofread Before Submitting

College students often wonder whether spelling and grammatical mistakes count in the grading of a paper. The answer is yes, they do—even if not "officially." A sloppy, typo-infested paper signals that you, the author, don't respect your work enough to have reread it and corrected errors. And if you don't respect the work, it's likely that your professor won't respect it much either.

Your computer spell-check will catch some blatant errors, but don't rely on it entirely, as it won't flag words that are spelled correctly but don't belong. (For example, a spell-check program will not catch the problematic "tent" in the phrase "economists tent to favor," even though you meant "tend.") To make sure your essay is clean of errors, read it aloud. This way you're likely to notice if a word is incorrectly typed, missing, or repeated. Another way to catch mistakes is to read your essay backward sentence by sentence. This forces you to focus on the words themselves rather than your expectations of what was written. And it's always a good idea to have someone else read the paper before you hand it in. The fresh set of eyes will see much that you missed.

WHO WOULD'VE THOUGHT?

Always make a copy of the paper that you submit to your professor. If you e-mail the paper, e-mail a copy to yourself as well. This might provide useful evidence to show that you did send out the paper as you said. And if your e-mail program provides this option, request either a "received" or "read" receipt so you can confirm that your instructor at least received your e-mail.

Hand in the Paper on Time or Earlier

Don't wait until the last day to get your paper ready; emergencies have a habit of getting in the way. And professors appreciate papers that are delivered to them early. It can only help your grade.

CHECKLIST FOR WRITING THE RESEARCH PAPER

- Have I chosen a topic that interests me?
- Have I done the preliminary research to determine if this is a good choice?
- Have I narrowed the scope and run it past my professor?
- Have I developed a clear thesis?
- Have I written a preliminary outline?
- Did I begin writing the paper in sufficient time?
- Did I write and rewrite several drafts of the paper?
- Did I revise and revise, and when I finished, did I go back and revise it again?
- Did I proofread the paper carefully?
- Have I submitted the paper on time, retaining a copy for myself?

AND REMEMBER . . .

You realize, correctly, that a solid education is a reward in itself. And you also, again correctly, expect your college education to serve as the path to a successful career. To follow that path, you need good grades. As we note throughout the chapter, you'll find many resources, both online and on campus, to help you perform at your best in school. But to get those good grades, you do have to commit yourself to focused and consistent study and completion of homework along with developing your skills at writing research papers. It also helps to master strategies for performing well on exams, as we'll see in our next chapter.

You can score higher on your tests by learning key test-taking strategies, which include surveying the test before answering questions, navigating short-answer exams, mastering the essential elements of essay exams, and subjecting your exam to careful review.

At the Test: Strategies for Your Brain and Body

YOU'VE STUDIED. You know the material cold. But the moment the blue answer book is placed on your desk and you're handed the exam, dread sets in. Your heart gallops, your shoulders tense, and your mind goes blank. You can't think straight, and the answers you knew so well ten minutes earlier have vanished.

This is not an uncommon scenario. An even more frequent occurrence is students who don't panic during tests but, nonetheless, perform poorly despite knowing the material. This is especially common among community college students, many of whom haven't taken school exams for some time. What these students need to improve is their test-taking skills.

Test-taking skills can be learned. That's why companies make millions of dollars tutoring students from kindergarten through medical school on how to improve their scores on standardized tests. Let's be clear, though: no matter how many test-taking tricks you have up your sleeve, *there is no substitute for studying*. But if you've done the requisite learning, improved test-taking skills lead to improved grades.

This chapter will walk you through the process and strategies of successful test taking, from before the test through the exam itself and afterward.

BEFORE YOU ANSWER THE FIRST QUESTION

An exam can be passed or failed before you even write the first answer. A few steps can help tilt the scales in favor of a positive score.

Arrive Prepared

Getting ready for the exam begins the night before. We're not referring here to the obvious preparation of studying, but the gathering of tools. Pack one or two working pens, a calculator if necessary, a wristwatch, and pencils if your answers will be submitted on Scantron forms. You might be too flustered on the day of the test to remember all these items, so stow them in your bag the night before.

Get enough sleep. This, too, is part of smart test preparation. We noted previously how insufficient sleep hampers thinking; a tired brain is an impaired brain. And eat a light, preferably high-protein breakfast. You want to arrive to the exam neither sluggish nor hungry. If you're a coffee drinker, go for it. Studies do suggest that the caffeine buzz jolts mental activity.[1]

Arrive Early

Not a term goes by in which students don't walk into a test late, leaving them with less time to complete the exam and the risk of having missed important test instructions. Don't join this group. In fact, you should plan to arrive not just in time, but early. For one thing, unexpected delays—traffic, parking problems, forgotten wallets, changed exam rooms, and so on—are a fact of life. In addition, arriving early allows you to choose a comfortable seat, get acclimated to the room, set out your test materials, and—if it doesn't make you nervous—get last-minute clarification from other students about material you found confusing.

Exercises for Reducing Anxiety

Most people are somewhat anxious when they're tested. The anxiety is not only normal, but even beneficial: the surge of adrenaline makes you more alert and improves test performance. Some people, however, get *very* anxious and reach a level of agitation that impedes their ability to answer questions they otherwise could.

FROM THE AUTHORS' FILES

Panic is a response to anxiety and fear. It's the frantic feeling that you can't control your emotional response. I understand the anxiety about tests. In fact, taking tests makes me very nervous. What I've learned to control is the panic, the awful—and self-fulfilling—feeling that I'll get flustered and won't be able to control my fluster. So don't worry about being worried about the test on your desk. There are psychological games you can play to calm yourself. One thing I do is recall other instances where I imagined myself messing up and how this would have a terrible impact in my life when, in fact, I didn't do badly and even if I had, the consequences would hardly have been tragic. Nothing that happens in class is worth your panic—there will be another test, another paper, another chance. *JH*

Do you, too, get "stressed out" when taking tests? Then learn how to relax. Psychologists offer various techniques for reducing anxiety rapidly, and you should try out several to see which works best for you. A survey of legitimate Web sites, such as Penn State's site about test anxiety at http://istudy.psu.edu/FirstYearModules/TestTaking/Test-Information.html, will turn up some of these proven strategies. These include closing your eyes for a few moments and taking deep breaths. Many suggest visualizations, imagining yourself working your way steadily through the exam. Pep talks help, too: "I know the material, and I will ace this exam."

Having an extra minute or two to engage in anxiety-reducing exercises is yet another reason to arrive early for the exam.

WHO WOULD'VE THOUGHT?

One helpful way to reduce stress is laughter. Laughing reduces the level of stress-related hormones such as cortisol and dopamine. And if you can manage a good belly laugh, you'll exercise your diaphragm and relax your muscles. Anxiety makes our challenges seem more threatening than they are; humor gives us an alternative, positive perspective. So exchange a joke before the exam, or think of something funny. A smile will go a long way in reducing stress.[2]

Pay Close Attention to Directions (Written And Oral)

What can be more frustrating than messing up on an exam that you'd have received an A on if you had paid closer attention to the instructions? Often, it's precisely because you're so on top of the material that you jump right in and begin answering questions—only not the questions being asked. *Never* assume you know what you're required to do on a test. When the instructor presents the instructions, listen carefully, even if you think you know what will be said. Read the instructions to each part of the exam thoroughly, even if you think you know what they will be. And if you aren't sure what's expected of you, ask. Your grade depends on answering the exam's questions, not your own.

And please make sure your name is on the answer booklet or answer page. Obvious?

You'd think so, but students often overlook this. In fact, do this first, so you don't forget later. An unnamed answer sheet can result in you not getting credit for taking the exam.

Examine the Entire Test Before You Begin

Students typically start writing as soon as they're handed the exam, beginning with question 1, moving on to question 2, and going straight through to the end. This is not the best strategy.

When you get your exam and read the instructions, the first thing to do is peruse the entire exam. This will give you an immediate feel for the sort of questions you'll have to answer and the length of the test and allows you to determine how you'll allocate your time to the different sections. Don't think that first reading through the entire test is wasting precious minutes. On the contrary, this quick overview will end up saving you time and mistakes.

A typical test will cover the material in more than one way. In particular, most short-answer tests contain some of the answers to their own questions in another part of the test. Look over the stems of the multiple-choice questions (not the choices offered as answers), see what topics are covered in the true/false questions and the matching questions, and note what you're asked to discuss in the essay. Now when you get to a tricky question, you'll know where in the test you can look for help.

Budget Your Time

College exams nearly always have time limits. Therefore, one of the main challenges of test taking is determining how much time to spend on the different questions. Mismanage your time allowance, and you'll find yourself rushing through questions worth lots of points—questions you'd otherwise have answered thoroughly. Note which problems are worth the most points, and allocate your time accordingly. Decide how you'll divide your time between the short answers and the essay question. Budget your time intelligently, and *you*—not the clock—will be in control of the exam.

Answer the Easy Questions First

When you read through the test, mark the questions you think will be "easy." Then answer those questions first, especially the easier questions with the most points. This has a twofold benefit: you build your confidence and put yourself in a positive frame for the other questions, and you avoid squandering precious time on difficult problems that show up early in the exam.

As far as those difficult questions that stump you, read each twice, and set a time limit for solving them. If the time expires and you're still unable to come up with the correct answer, take your best guess and move on. If you need to provide a completion, or fill-in-the-blank answer, write what you do know and continue on. Don't linger on turf that will remain dry no matter how hard you squeeze it.

ANSWERING EXAM QUESTIONS

By and large, your exams will be any combination of short-answer and essay questions. There are different strategies for answering each type of question, but one principle is common to both: read the question carefully!

Short-Answer Questions

Throughout college, across your courses, you're bound to take short-answer exams.

Honing your skills at these tests will go a long way toward doing well in school. Below are some suggestions for the various short-answer exams you'll be meeting.

True/False Questions

This category of questions is the student's best friend. After all, you could answer any number of the questions correctly by simply flipping a coin. If you know anything at all about the subject, your chance of answering most of the questions correctly should be even higher. There are, in addition, cues that can point you to the right answer.

- Be wary of words such as "never," "always," and "only." These words are absolutes and allow no exceptions. If you can think of one exception, the answer is false. And because professors recognize the possibility of an exception to their statement, they probably intended the statement to be false. But, mind you, we said "probably," not "always." There are exceptions: occasionally, "always" and "never" statements are true. Above all, go with the answer you're convinced is correct.
- Remember the law of conjunction. For a statement to be true, each part of it must be true. Some teachers will make only part of

a sentence true to catch the careless. For example, "Washington, D.C., is the capital of the United States, and Milan is the capital of Italy" is a false statement.

Multiple-Choice Questions (and Matching)

The SAT, the ACT, the GRE, the LSAT—indeed, nearly all standardized tests—rely heavily on multiple-choice questions. No wonder companies in the tutoring business focus on teaching tactics for answering multiple-choice questions. Some of the best of these hints are available, at no cost, on the Web.

Here are two useful suggestions for succeeding on multiple-choice tests:

- After you read the question, put your hand over the choices offered as answers. You want to avoid reading an option that seems correct and, as a result, get locked in to that answer before you seriously consider the alternatives. Instead, decide what you think the answer should be, and then select the choice that's most similar to your own.
- The key to doing well on multiple-choice questions is intelligent guessing. Nearly always your test score depends on how many questions you've answered correctly, so it makes sense to answer all the questions. If you don't know the answer, eliminate the obvious wrong answers, and choose the most reasonable option of the remaining alternatives.

Matching questions are best thought of as a form of multiple-choice question. Most of the tips that apply to multiple-choice questions apply to them as well. Here, too, for example, first match those pairs that you are sure of, and then use the process of elimination to answer the rest.

Completions

Something is usually better than nothing, so even if you can't fully answer the question, write down what you know instead of leaving the question blank. Many teachers award partial credit if you demonstrate at least some inkling of the answer. A more common error is to write too much rather than too little. You might want to impress your instructor with how much you know, but if what you add is false, you'll lose points rather than gain them. Usually a word or short phrase will do. Just answer the question fully and then stop.

A SHORT MULTIPLE TUTORIAL ON MULTIPLE ANSWERS

- Often, the choice that is couched in the most general terms is the correct answer. For example, suppose the choices for the definition of a table are: A) an object with four 2x2 legs; B) an object two feet high and three feet wide; C) an article of furniture consisting of a flat, slablike top supported on one or more legs or other supports; D) a rectangular piece of wood usually of several feet surrounded by chairs and used for eating. Which do you think is the correct answer? The correct answer is C, the most general and inclusive of these choices.
- When given a range of numbers, the correct answer is most often somewhere between the extremes. For example: Adults have how many teeth? A) 7; B) 15; C) 32; D) 54. Answer? C. (B would have been the other reasonable guess.)
- When two responses are opposite, one of them is probably correct.

Essay Questions

Knowing how to write a formidable essay is essential for superior grades. The following are effective tips to help you achieve better grades on essay exams.

Read the Entire Question

As with the short-answer part of the test, first read through all the essay questions. Jot down key words, facts, and associations that come to mind as you consider the question; you may forget them later when you're under time pressure. Then read each question carefully. Don't assume you know what the question is asking without fully reading it.

Budget Your Time

If you're asked to write more than one essay, budget how much time you want to spend on each question and keep to your plan. It's too easy to get carried away with your first essay and then panic because you left not nearly enough time for the next one and are limited to scribbling a sentence or two as your essay.

Write an Outline

Do this on scratch paper if allowed or somewhere in your test booklet. You might think this will cost you precious time, but, in fact, outlining saves you time. Writing with the hope that you'll happen upon the right answer is both time-consuming and futile. With an outline in front of you, your essay will be organized and clear. You'll know where you're going and how you'll get there.

DIGGING DEEPER

Your first and last sentences will probably be read even more carefully than any other in your essay. So give them some punch. Students regularly began their essays spinning their wheels to get started and jot down vague generalities. Answering an essay question on World War II, say, they'll begin with something like "War has plagued mankind for thousands of years," and end with another platitude such as "War will continue to plague mankind...." Instead of these generalities, begin with a clear thesis statement that makes a strong point, such as, "Although war has plagued mankind for thousands of years, WWII was unique in that it began with an alliance of powers that spread from the Pacific to the Atlantic." End with a strong sentence as well. Make a good first and last impression.

There are a multitude of Web sites offering college students advice on essay writing. Two good ones are http://owl.english.purdue.edu/handouts/general/gl_essay.html, which provides detailed guidance on organizational patterns for essays, and http://mockingbird.creighton.edu/REDOER, which, along with other suggestions, provides memory tactics for writing essays.

INSTRUCTIONS FOR INSTRUCTIONAL WORDS

Pay attention to the words in the essay question's instructions to make sure that you are doing what the question asks.

Analyze	Break into separate parts and discuss, examine, or interpret each part.
Compare	Show similarities (and differences).
Contrast	Emphasize the differences.
Criticize	Analyze and then evaluate.
Define	Give an accurate and specific meaning.
Describe	Provide a detailed account. List characteristics, qualities, and context.
Diagram	Provide a chart or sketch with accompanying explanations.
Discuss	Talk about important characteristics, main points, and relevant background.
Evaluate	Note the merits, strengths, weaknesses, advantages, or limitations of the topic. Make sure to provide support for your position.
Explain	Give facts, details, and reasons that make the idea clear and understandable.
Illustrate	Give concrete examples that clarify a point.
Justify	Give reasons that support an action, event, or policy.
Outline	Describe main ideas, characteristics, or events (usually with little elaboration).
Prove	Support with facts. Demonstrate that a concept or theory is correct, logical, or valid.
Relate	Discuss the connection, correlation, relationships, and points of association among ideas and facts.
State	Explain precisely.
Summarize	Give a brief account but avoid unnecessary details.
Trace	Describe the development of a trend, event, or process in chronological order.

Answer the Question Asked

It seems obvious, but the professor is looking to evaluate your understanding of specific topics. Focus your essay on those concepts—not the issue you wish you were asked.

LENGTH AND STRUCTURE

Although there are many variables that could affect the length of your essay (the duration of the exam, the number of essay questions, and so on), in general, you should aim for a three- to five-paragraph answer.

The first paragraph should be your introduction, which will include your thesis. You can turn part of the question itself into your thesis. For example, if your essay asks, "Trace the rise of Latino theatre in the United States," you might begin with "Although there have been Latino theatrical troops in the United States from as early as the beginning of the twentieth century, we can really trace the rise of the Latino theatre in the last three decades."

In the next paragraphs, you will want to use specific examples and details to support your thesis. Your final paragraph will summarize the main points you have raised and perhaps reiterate your thesis statement.

NOTE THE MOST ESSENTIAL IDEAS FIRST

Make sure your strongest ideas are the ones your instructors see first. If they are immediately persuaded you understand the material, they're likely to be more sympathetic as they read the rest of your essay.

GENERALIZE WHEN NECESSARY

You want to avoid making false statements that will cost you points. So when you aren't sure about a specific fact, write more generally. It's better to say "In the early years of the nineteenth century" than "In 1803" if you aren't sure of the year.

AFTER COMPLETING THE TEST

Although you might feel exhausted and ready to put this test behind you, hold on.

Before Submitting Your Exam

Once you've completed your exam, realize that you have worked hard. You might as well invest a few more minutes to assure your winning grade.

Review Your Answers Before You Hand Them In

No matter how meticulous you think you've been, take a few minutes to go over your answers. Careless mistakes are commonplace. Make sure you've answered every question. Check for misplaced decimals. Make sure your letter answers are legible (the "c" doesn't look like an "e" and the "a" won't be read as a "d"). There's a popular notion that you should always stick with your first choice, but if you have a good reason to lean toward a different choice, by all means change your answer.

Go Back to Difficult Questions

Now that you've completed the test, your memory might have been jogged. You might have come upon information that will convince you to change an answer or tell you what you need to know to answer the question that baffled you earlier.

Take the Time to Reread Your Essay

As you read over your essay one last time, you'll often find misspelled words, omitted words, dates incorrectly noted (for example, 1984 instead of 1948), needed transitional phrases, and other oversights. A sloppy essay invites a lower grade. Reread what you've written before submitting.

And, Finally, After The Test

Your graded test is feedback. It's neither a measurement of your worth as a student nor an evaluation of your intelligence. As hard as it might seem—especially if you messed up on the exam—learn to use the test results as a learning opportunity.

As with all learning tools, it's best to go over the material when it's still fresh in your mind. Review the answers you got wrong, and learn what would make them right. Examine your teacher's comments on your essay; this way, you'll know what's expected of you on the next test. Note if the questions you got wrong derived mainly from the text or the lectures; this way, you'll know where to concentrate for future exams. If you don't understand why an answer was marked wrong, arrange to discuss this with your instructor.

There's one more reason to review a graded test. Your instructor might have made a mistake in grading your exam, and he or she will be happy to rectify any mistake made in calculating your grade.

AND REMEMBER...

Your grades are the most relied-upon measure of your academic performance in school. While there are some factors beyond your control, how well you do is largely up to you. As we've seen, achieving superior grades requires smart and systematic studying, learning how to write effectively, and mastering helpful test-taking strategies. Succeeding at these challenges will require overcoming bad habits, but make the effort, and getting good grades will become a recurring, welcome experience.

GET GOING

PART THREE

College activities outside the classroom can enhance your college experience, strengthen your résumé, and develop personal talents that will reward you for your entire life.

So You Want to Join the Circus: Extracurricular Activities, Internships, and Study Abroad

THE CLASSROOM ISN'T THE ONLY PLACE on campus for learning. Nor is it the only place for developing rewarding relationships with other students. In fact, college life teems outside the classroom. Here you'll find an array of activities—educational, social, civic-minded, artistic, and athletic—that will make your college experience that much richer. In this chapter, we'll have a look at extracurricular activities as well as internships and study abroad programs, three opportunities that can significantly enrich your years at community college.

EXTRACURRICULAR ACTIVITIES

The term *extracurricular* makes you think of luxury add-ons, like extra credit, icing on the cake, pastimes you can really do without. And it's true you can graduate college by only showing up to class, passing your exams, and making a fast getaway. But why limit yourself to that? Why miss a vital part of the college experience? Extracurricular pursuits help you forge lasting connections and create new, lifelong friendships. By participating in these activities, you'll expand your set of skills, learning things about yourself you never knew, and build your résumé. And last, but surely not least, extracurricular activities are fun.

Why not join? The most common excuse is time. Given your work schedule, your family obligations, and schoolwork, you conclude you have no time to devote to these "recreations." But be honest with yourself here. Add up the week's hours spent watching television, Web surfing, idle telephone chattering, and magazine skimming. You need time for these pleasures, sure, but certainly you can trade some of those hours to worthwhile campus extracurricular programs as well. See this as an important aspect of being in college, and you can make time for it all.

Participation in these activities is especially important for you precisely because, not living on campus (as is true of most community college students), you might feel isolated, as though you don't fully belong. By integrating campus activities into your social life, you develop a genuine sense of affiliation to your school and your fellow students.

Let's take a look at the large menu of extracurricular options available to you.

School Events

Want to see a movie? Does "free" sound appealing? How about something a little different from the usual Hollywood blockbusters everyone else is watching? A variety of clubs on campus show films and documentaries you won't see anywhere else, all open to the college community and usually at no cost. The presentation might also be accompanied by a talk that provides intriguing insights about the subject of the film and its production.

DIGGING DEEPER

Lakeland Community College in Ohio offers an International Film Festival, Bellevue Community College in Washington offers an annual American Indian Film Festival, and Tidewater Community College in Virginia has hosted the Annual Virginia Festival of Jewish Film, just to list a few. Find out what your college has in the works.

Movies are just one example of the countless events on campus that are regularly available to students. Throughout the year, you'll be greeted with a busy menu to choose from: lectures from visiting experts on everything from art to zoology, dance performances, musical performances in all genres, theater, debates, and poetry readings. Drop in on some of these events when you can, and be open to new experiences. Don't assume you know what you'll enjoy; you might be in for a pleasant surprise.

Your college will offer a range of annual events such as International Week, Political Activism Week, Year End Picnics—each an opportunity for you to have fun, be introduced to new ideas, and meet many of your professors and your fellow classmates in a less formal setting.

How do you find out what's happening on campus? Look for posters along the walls of the hallways and bulletin boards across campus. Check out the student center, where scheduled events are always posted. Look at your e-mail. Most college events are publicized with a college-wide electronic blast. Check your college newspaper for announcements. Listen to word-of-mouth news. Pay attention; the information is all around you.

Clubs

If you talk to college graduates about their most rewarding experiences in school, their membership in a club is sure to be toward the top of the list.

The reasons for joining a club are many, and each would be persuasive on its own. Consider the following.

You'll Learn a New Skill or Develop One That Has Been Hiding

Think you've got a bit of the talent of a Will Smith, Brad Pitt, or Beyoncé lurking inside you? Well, you might, but you won't find out unless you give that talent a chance to emerge. Sign up to audition for a school play. Perhaps you'll be offered the lead. Is it poetry that interests you or writing short stories, songs, or news articles? There's a literary magazine waiting to discuss your work and a newspaper staff who'd love to see your contributions. Curious about astronomy? Enjoy chess? Enthusiastic about salsa? There might be a club of like-minded students who share your passion. And if you have a yearning for politics, student government offers many opportunities for running for office and developing your political, oratory, and interpersonal skills.

WHO WOULD'VE THOUGHT?

Belonging to a club often provides unexpected benefits. For example, as a member of the debate team, you'll get to travel to other parts of the country and meet people you'd otherwise never cross paths with. And in some schools, you can actually get paid for working in positions in student government. These additional perks certainly aren't your objective in participating, but they're a welcome addition when they come your way.

From the spectrum of clubs and organizations active in your school, consider one that allows you to explore a talent or interest that's been submerged, waiting to burst forth. You might never get this opportunity again, so go for it.

FROM THE AUTHORS' FILES

Back in college, I had this notion that I had the makings of a superior chess player. After all, I soundly beat most of my cousins and a few of my uncles. So I tried out for the chess club. Well, I didn't come close to making the team. But I did get to hang out with fellow chess players and spent many delightful hours in the cafeteria practicing new openings. On the other hand, I never supposed I had a particular interest in films, but the film club showed me otherwise. I was introduced to movies from directors I'd never heard of from countries with names I'd only seen on maps. Those viewings and discussions resulted in a lifelong interest. And I see this sort of experience happen all the time with my students. They join the acting club on a whim or write for magazines and newspapers—try out all sorts of activities—and develop passions I know they will sustain—and that will sustain them—for the rest of their lives. *JH*

You'll Make Important Connections and New Friends

Clubs and organizations provide their members with a special camaraderie. You're all there because you want to be, sharing similar interests and working for the same cause. The ties you make there can serve you years later.

As you're no doubt aware, connections are a significant factor in the development of one's career. *Who* you know might not be as important as *what* you know, but it sure does help. These links can be direct if a club is affiliated with your target profession—for example, someone in the automotive club ends up owning a garage and asks if you're interested in a job as associate manager. But connections also reach out in unexpected directions: it might not be the fellow who served with you in the student senate who gets you that interview at the bank but his uncle, the bank's supervisor.

Moreover, the associations you establish as a club member extend beyond your relationships with fellow college students. Clubs often invite guest speakers from associated industries—for example, a TV anchor to talk to the media club or a CEO of a local company to address the business club. These events are an excellent opportunity to network with someone of influence in the field you are pursuing.

We've highlighted the potential career benefits of extracurricular club participation, but the social relationships that await you are no less satisfying. Now you can go beyond the quick "how are you" and "see you around" exchanged before and after class and initiate and sustain genuine friendships; often the deepest camaraderie comes from working together on a project of shared interest.

Doing Good

Many college clubs and organizations are dedicated not to personal interests but to helping others. Some work for global and national causes such as global warming and refugee aid, and others are dedicated to meeting the needs of the local community. They organize activities such as blood drives or offer services such as tutoring for children with special needs.

Joining one of these clubs provides a long list of personal rewards that includes useful experience in the nonprofit sector. But perhaps the best reason of all for joining a club devoted to social assistance is simply for the sake of decency: you want to help others, and you want to make a difference.

Career Building

One immediate benefit of participating in a college club is rather practical: a more appealing résumé.

Here's the reality. Your résumé will stand out if, along with a strong GPA, you can demonstrate participation in an extracurricular club; it will stand out even more if you can highlight a leadership position in that organization. Active and commendable involvement in a club will boost your chances to receive a scholarship, academic honors, and acceptance to a four-year college.

Club participation will also improve your job search. Employers are looking for employees who are well-rounded team players with leadership skills and a commitment to self-development. Active participation in a club demonstrates those desired qualities.

You'll Have Fun

We've saved this for last, but it's certainly not the least of the good reasons for getting involved in a college organization. College life shouldn't be only about studying, classes, and exams. Clubs are an oasis from the stress. Here you can hang out with your friends, unwind, discover stimulating challenges, and share some well-deserved laughs.

CHECKLIST FOR HOW TO GET INVOLVED

- Find out what's happening on and off campus by keeping up with print announcements and e-mails.
- If you're curious about a club, get in touch with a member, and stop by one of its meetings.
- Check your campus e-mail regularly to learn about upcoming events.
- Attend college information fairs, talk to members of various clubs, and read their brochures.
- Find out about religious, social, or political clubs if that's where your interest lies. They are always open to new members and volunteers.

- Visit the fitness center, and pick up a schedule of athletic clubs and activities.
- Consider starting your own club. If you have a new obsession with clowning, say, why not organize a club for fellow clowns? Or start a club with those who share your love for fencing, meditation, sewing, art films, or Ancient Greek? Stop by your school's student activities office to find out how to organize a new club.

College Sports and Physical Activity

A surprising number of students visit the school gym on their first tour of the school and never return. But here's a resource you ought to consider making part of your on-campus routine.

No one needs to hear again about the benefits of physical exercise. But now, with a gymnasium right near your history class, you can generate that needed sweat without losing sweat. And, unlike expensive gyms, the cost of this resource is zero—students can use the facilities for free!

Stop by the physical education or health and wellness department at your school or visit their site online to see when the various facilities are restricted to team use and when they are available to all staff and students. Then take your run around the track. Or on the treadmill. Or work out in the weight room. Don't have a tennis court in your backyard? Need to drive to get to a basketball court? No problem. There's one waiting for you on campus. Some colleges even offer a pool.

It's a good idea to schedule some physical activity into the time you're on campus. You might find an hour for exercise before classes, during a break, or later, when you've finished your class day. This is a great way to refresh yourself and improve your health in the bargain.

If you have a talent for a sport, consider joining an athletic team. Don't assume you aren't good enough. Try out for your college baseball, soccer, basketball, or swimming team or another of the various teams your college features. And remember that you don't have to be on the varsity team to play sports. You can always join an informal pickup basketball game or the three students on the handball court waiting for a fourth. College athletics is yet another wonderful way to meet your fellow students.

INTERNSHIPS

One of the best educational activities outside the classroom is also one of the most rewarding: interning. This, too, is a terrific opportunity that so many community college students are unaware they are eligible for. Be resourceful and determined, and you'll be among the select students who make the most of these waiting internships.

Am I Becoming a Doctor?

You do not have to be enrolled in a premedical program to be an intern. An internship is, essentially, work for a profit or nonprofit organization as arranged by the college or specific department within the college, either for credit or not. Internships are usually available to students who are already halfway through their course work and are rarely available to entering freshmen.

DIGGING DEEPER

Your college can supply you with helpful addresses of organizations to contact for an internship. Check with the department of your major as well to see if there's an internship related to your target career. For a comprehensive list of internships in the nonprofit arena, visit http://www.idealist.org.

Benefits

Although the typical internship does not pay students a salary, other rewards make the time and effort well worth it. First, there's no better way for you to learn about a business or profession than from the inside. If you're considering a career in the field, you'll now have a far more realistic sense of the daily work life in that industry. As a result, you may become even more enthusiastic about your career goals than you were to begin with (or, conversely, your internship experience might lead you to change your major!).

Internships are available for most careers, from film to medicine to paralegal work. But availability shouldn't be the only criterion you consider when choosing an internship. Ask yourself what you want to gain from the experience. For example, suppose you're thinking of a career in media production and have an opportunity to work for a large television producer, say MTV. The company bubbles with energy, is housed in a marvelous facility, and lets you work with lots of like-minded people. In addition, you also might come into contact with senior managers who might further your career when you graduate from college. But also recognize that in these large, established companies, you aren't likely to get much hands-on training. You're more likely to be sent out to buy the coffee for a staff meeting than sent out to work on a project. On the other hand, interning at a small enterprise with little name recognition might mean you'll be taught and get to practice a range of skills that will serve you well when you enter the marketplace. Either way, though, the internship allows you to include genuine work experience on your résumé, and that will certainly help you continue your education or secure that first postgraduation job.

STUDY ABROAD

In recent years, many community colleges have initiated study abroad programs. If possible, don't miss out on this extraordinary experience. Although many community college students have responsibilities that preclude studying abroad, if your school offers the opportunity, give it serious consideration.

What Study Abroad Entails

Living in a foreign country for an extended period of time is far different than visiting there as a tourist. As part of a college program, you'll either be attending classes at an affiliated college in another country or working at some organization, and perhaps living with a local family. In any case, your own daily routine will be integrated into the lives of those around you. You'll learn the language, attitudes, and local lifestyle as no tourist can. And you'll learn about yourself: without the familiar social support of back home, you'll discover much about your internal resources.

Different Types and Time Frames

There is no one-size-fits-all study abroad program. These programs come in different arrangements, with different goals and different time frames. Some focus on history with an emphasis on the city you are staying in, such as California's Coast Community College's summer program in London, which focuses on British history of the late Middle Ages. The advantage here is that you won't have the language to worry about! Other programs will explore an area that might enhance both your understanding of global issues as well as your future career, such as the intersession program in China from Rockland Community College in New York, which offers (among other courses) Health Care in China and awards three nursing credits. If you want to acquire a new language, you might be interested in a program such as Hawaii's Kapi'olani Community College's study abroad program in France, Japan, or China. These language programs might schedule four hours of language study in the morning followed by cultural outings in the afternoon.

The length of time of study abroad programs varies greatly. In the three programs mentioned above, the Coast program lasts a month, Rockland's intersession program is just two weeks, and Kapi'olani's is a full year. You need to research what your campus offers and how it may coincide with your goals and requirements.

TEN REASONS TO STUDY ABROAD

1. Study abroad is an extraordinary opportunity to learn about another culture firsthand.
2. Study abroad helps you learn about yourself as you couldn't by staying home.
3. Study abroad is a terrific way to travel—alone or with new friends, and often at less cost.
4. Study abroad helps you develop skills you'd never get from the classroom alone.
5. Study abroad is the best way to learn a new language or practice one you've been studying.
6. Study abroad is a wonderful way to make friends around the world.

7. Study abroad expands your view and understanding of the world.
8. Study abroad gives you a refreshing break from your regular college routine.
9. Study abroad provides new ideas for your career along with opportunities.
10. Study abroad will enhance your résumé and the value of your degree.

Cost

Study abroad programs are not cheap but are also probably less expensive than you might suppose. Most provide scholarships or direct financial aid sources that can help pay all or a portion of your costs.

DIGGING DEEPER

If you are interested in studying abroad, make sure to look into all the numerous scholarship opportunities available for community college students. Your own college might provide financial resources, as do national initiatives such as the Benjamin A. Gilman International Scholarship Program (see http://www.iie.org/programs/gilman/overview/overview.html) or the American Institute for Foreign Study (AIFS) Scholarship (see http://www.aifsabroad.com/scholarships.asp).

And as you'll usually receive college credit for your study abroad, you can use at least some of your federal and state financial aid toward your trip. Altogether not a bad deal!

AND REMEMBER...

A satisfying college career involves more than just absorbing information. You want to be fully engaged. Extracurricular activities, internships, and study abroad programs offer a challenge to stretch yourself, nourish new talents and develop old ones, and contribute to others in the process. And beyond the career benefits these activities offer are the equally satisfying social connections you'll make. Don't deprive yourself of a complete college experience. Get involved!

To assure a smooth transfer to a four-year school, you will need a thorough understanding of the requirements for transfer and a willingness to undertake an active role in the process.

Help Carrying Your Luggage: Transferring to a Four-Year School

IF YOU ARE LIKE MANY STUDENTS entering community college, you're thinking of eventually going on for a bachelor's degree from a four-year college.

The unhappy reality is that most students who plan to transfer to four-year schools don't.[1] But *you* can be among those who do succeed in making the transition. It will take ongoing confidence in yourself, continued optimism, and, as important, a thorough understanding of the transition process. But don't wait until your final semester in college before dealing with the complex issues of transfer; you should begin thinking about transfer in your first term in school.

Before we look at both the approach and factual information you'll need to transfer successfully, we should point out that success is in your control. Four-year colleges want you! These institutions are eager to increase enrollment, and they are especially eager to attract good students. They recognize that community college students who complete their degrees present an outstanding pool of potential students. They recognize, too, that, in these difficult economic times and with the high cost of college rising even higher, more and more capable students are choosing to spend their first years at a community college primarily for financial reasons. Upper-division institutions appreciate that community college transfer students have been through the college process and have proved they're capable of handling its stresses and demands and meet their academic challenges.

However, one of the main obstacles community college students face when considering transfer to a four-year college is psychological. They worry that they lack the skills to graduate with that bachelor's degree. If that's your concern as well—and it's a reasonable concern—perhaps this piece of news will help allay your fears: the graduation rate of two-year students who transfer to senior colleges is as good as or better than that of students who began as freshmen at these four-year schools.[2] Moreover, transfer students generally do as well as or better academically than students who have been at their four-year school from the beginning. No wonder four-year colleges have begun to actively court community college students—they know that students like you will excel at their schools.

We can't supply the necessary determination—that's up to you. But even with the right attitude, you won't transfer effectively unless you become familiar with the terminology and steps required. Let's review these essential aspects of the transfer process.

THE FOUNDATIONS OF YOUR TRANSFER

The ins and outs of transferring are not difficult but demand that a foundation is in place before you can move forward.

Terminology

There are a number of terms that you need to be familiar with that will inform any discussion you may have about transferring.

Transfer Programs

Transfer programs are community college programs designed to ready students for their move to a four-year college. Ideally, after you have completed an AA or AS degree of between approximately sixty and seventy credits, you can enroll as an entering junior in an upper-division school, or at least transfer as many credits as possible.

Joint Programs

Joint programs are established by two educational institutions, with both institutions awarding credits for classes completed. A student who, say, undertook a joint program in criminal justice by completing the prescribed two years of course work with an adequate grade point average at a community college is automatically eligible for the second part of the program at the partnering four-year school. Because joint programs are designed by both schools, community college students can move on seamlessly to the final two years of course work.

Articulation Agreements

An articulation agreement is a document that recognizes the equivalence of a community college program and a similar program in the participating four-year school. Representatives of each institution compare the respective courses in their school's program to determine which courses are comparable and will be granted credit. They also determine which courses meet the requirement toward the major or will count as an elective credit. This consensus is formalized as an articulation agreement. If you go to a school that has an articulation agreement with a four-year college in your area of study, the articulation agreement will allow you to transfer there as a junior.

DIGGING DEEPER

Many states are now passing legislation mandating transferability and articulation. This will go a long way toward easing the transfer process for community college students. Check to see if your state has legislation governing articulation for community college students at http://www.aacrao.org/pro_development/transfer.cfm.

Complete Your Degree Requirements

Make sure you've completed your required courses before you apply for transfer. And don't wait until the last moment to complete other college requirements such as writing-intensive classes. You may discover in your last semester that these needed classes aren't offered that term, delaying your graduation as a result.

Deal with Your Finances

Along with anxiety about their academic ability, community college students worry that they won't be able to afford tuition at a four-year college. As is the concern about ability, the anxiety about money is natural but can be addressed.

SCHOLARSHIP RESOURCES

Check out these online scholarship sources for transferring community college students:

http://www.thesalliemaefund.org/smfnew/scholarship/comm_ college_transfer.html

This site offers information on a scholarship program for Hispanic students.

http://www.hsf.net/scholarships.aspx?id=452

The Hispanic Scholarship Fund site has numerous scholarships in conjunction with corporations (for example, Nissan) for transferring students.

http://www.ptk.org/schol/schollisting.htm

This site lists all schools that offer scholarships to community college students who are members of Phi Theta Kappa, the honor society for community colleges.

And check out state Web sites, as there are numerous scholarship programs for every individual school.

Although it is true that, in general, four-year schools are more expensive than two-year schools, many public four-year colleges are still fairly reasonably priced. That is to say less expensive than you might imagine and probably within your grasp—even if it takes a little work to make it so. You may, of course, need to consider taking a loan, but, as we've noted, the investment in a college degree will pay off. In addition, there are numerous scholarships for which you might qualify. And schools are beginning to address the needs of transfer students more vigorously. For example, Morgan State University offers a Bridge Grant to students who earn at least twenty-four credits before transfer. The grant provides $1,000 each semester along with extra tuition scholarships if you have graduated with an associate's degree.

WHO WOULD'VE THOUGHT?

Some foundations have set aside money specifically for students who transfer from a community college to a four-year college. For example, over the past several years, the Jack Kent Cooke Foundation has awarded more than $24 million to transfer students. To find out about applying for this funding, visit http://www.jackkentcookefoundation.org/jkcf_web/home. aspx?Page=Main.

As always when applying for financial aid or scholarships, be cognizant of deadlines. If you apply late, you might be denied aid you'd otherwise receive. Remember to complete your FAFSA before March for the next academic year. And bear in mind, too, that the earlier you apply for admission and complete your financial aid application or renewal, the sooner you'll receive your award letter and learn how much financial aid you'll receive.

Pay Careful Attention to the Deadlines

The deadline for your financial aid application is but one of others you'll need to think about as you prepare to transfer. For example, because four-year schools have different time periods for application, you will need to find out when your application is due at the school or schools you'd like to attend. A late submission can cost you an entire semester. As always, be conservative in your judgment of the time you'll need to complete and submit your application. Remember that old rule of thumb: estimate how much time it will take and then double it.

ESSENTIAL STEPS FOR TRANSFER

In many cases, for many students, the transfer can be incredibly simple. If you are attending a state community college and plan on transferring to the same state's four-year institution that has the program you have studied and/or an articulation agreement with your school, you may need no more than to have your transcript sent over and wait for your acceptance letter. But if perhaps you are looking to enroll in a public institution in another state or a private college in your own state (or a public institution that doesn't have an articulation agreement with your school), take a deep breath: this will call for added research and dedication on your part. There are, in any case, essential steps you'll need to take to ensure that your submitted transcript will achieve a positive outcome.

Begin Paying Attention to the Transfer Process Immediately

Immediately means as soon as you begin your course work at your community college. Too many students wait until their third term or later before calculating how many transferable credits they have, only to find out they've taken nontransferable classes and need to make up those credits. It's an unfortunate fact that four-year schools and two-year schools do not work together nearly as well as they should for the benefit of students. Therefore, the sooner you know what is needed, the better you'll be able to tailor your curriculum choices for the school you wish to attend.

Study the College Catalogue

There are at least two college catalogues and Web sites you want to examine. The first is the catalogue or Web site of the community college you are presently attending. Along with vital information about your college's transfer policies, you'll discover here which offices in the college deal with transfer programs and the names of the staff members who can assist you.

FROM THE AUTHORS' FILES

Sometimes we can't embrace emotionally what we know makes sense for us logically. This is often the situation students face when it comes to transfer. We're so eager to take courses in our chosen area of study, but, in truth, we're often better off attaining a solid foundation in all areas of study. Taking courses in a narrow area of study can cause problems later on. Some courses don't transfer smoothly, and, in other cases, the school you transfer to may require you to enroll in an introductory class. Two of my students, eager to begin their careers in education, took classes in that field, neglecting courses in art, music, and foreign languages. This ultimately cost them additional years at their four-year school. The narrower your field of study for the first two years, the more limited your options for a successful transfer will be.

So when given the choice, opt for acquiring a good foundation rather than specialized courses with which to transfer. Then you will truly have the tools to soar as you travel on your educational journey. *DG*

The other catalogues and Web sites you'll be investigating belong to the four-year colleges you target as your transfer schools. In some cases, you might have a good idea early on which school this will be; because of financial, work, or family commitments, you might concentrate on a local, public four-year school with which your college articulates. On the other hand, if you have acquired an associate's degree in Liberal Arts and Sciences, which offers a wide choice of future study and career avenues, or if you have done extraordinarily well in your studies and have a choice of schools, you might want to research the catalogues of a number of senior college possibilities. As the time approaches to submit your transfer request, study the transfer sections of the catalogues and Web sites of your possible target four-year schools to see whom you can contact with your questions and for confirmation of your information.

Talk to an Advisor at Your College

Now that you've studied the catalogue, and the transfer information available on your college's Web site and that of your "target" college, arrange to speak with an advisor at your school. You'll need his or her expert advice on which courses have transferable credits and how best to structure your course work. Your advisor will be up on the latest developments and advise you wisely on which of your classes will transfer.

Have this conversation during your first semester. And have this conversation again and again, term after term, to make sure you're taking the right classes. In addition, as you get nearer to completing your courses and to graduation, your advisor can provide you with helpful resources linking you to four-year colleges: Web sites, scholarship opportunities, and even the names of people to talk to at your target four-year school. Don't worry about being a nag. It's your advisor's job to help you. Community colleges are committed to helping their students make the transition to a four-year college as fluid and smooth as possible.

But be aware that even a well-meaning advisor may not know all the nuances of your area of study, so make sure to double- and even triple-check with the chair of your department. To be certain you're on the right track, make inquiries, too, at the school to which you wish to transfer.

Do Your Research

Helpful transfer resources are available, but don't rely on any one of them alone. It will be your responsibility to obtain information and confirm the information you receive.

The good news is that much of this information is easily accessible. Many states provide online statewide databases that include course articulation agreements between public two-year colleges and public four-year colleges. Check out these sites regularly, as transfer policies are constantly updated.

TRANSFERRING FROM A TWO-YEAR TO A FOUR-YEAR SCHOOL

You can find a wealth of transfer information online. Here are a few sites that focus on various aspects of the process.

http://www.collegefish.org

This is a Web portal through which you can research colleges that might be a good fit for you. At this site you can also look up scholarship possibilities and their deadlines.

http://www.connectedu.net/corp/index.html

At this site you'll find a calendar with deadlines for college and financial aid applications and learn whether a selected four-year college will accept various transfer credits.

http://www.assist.org

This site provides information on transferring between California schools, but it also has important data that can be used by community college students anywhere.

http://www.collegeanswer.com/selecting/content/sel_cc_transfer.jsp

This site includes a great checklist for transferring from community college.

Access Other Resources

In addition to catalogues, college Web sites, and advisors, a host of other information resources is available to the community college student seeking to transfer to a four-year school.

For example, a growing number of community colleges sponsor

transfer fairs and workshops to help link students with public and private four-year colleges and universities. At these fairs you'll learn a good deal about how to transfer to four-year colleges—those you're considering and those you perhaps should be considering. In addition to facts about admission requirements and academic programs, you'll also learn about student housing, athletic programs, financial aid, employment resources after graduation, and much more.

But be aware that these fairs can be downright crowded. Don't expect to be able to visit each college booth at length; you need to allocate your time wisely. Therefore, prepare beforehand. Find out which colleges will be attending the fair. Your college will have the list, and often you can get that information on the Web as well. A quick survey of the various schools on the list will inform you which seem most compatible with your major, location, academic strength, "college culture," and other factors that matter to you. From the best candidates, choose several schools to visit at the fair. Be realistic: more than six or seven is probably too many.

What if you can't make the fair that day? Some colleges now host transfer fairs online. As part of their ongoing programs to provide information to potential community college transferees, many four-year schools offer online presentation videos and the contact information students need to follow up on their applications.

Another helpful resource to learn about transferring is college publications. Many community colleges regularly publish newsletters devoted specifically to transfer issues. Here you'll find relevant information about transferring in general but also columns devoted to transfer issues for particular majors and careers. Along with fairs and workshops, these publications, fliers, and newsletters are an excellent source of ongoing information.

Talk to an Advisor at the School You'd Like to Attend

As we've mentioned, if you're planning to attend a four-year school that is part of a larger system, you can concentrate on your upcoming finals and begin preparing for the first day at the new school. However, if you're planning to enroll in a school outside the system, you'll need to consider talking to an advisor at the college you'd like to attend.

If—and when—you have a pretty good idea of where you want to transfer, undertake a bit of reverse engineering. That is, work backward. Talk to the appropriate transfer advisor at that four-year school, and build your community college course work to meet your target school's requirements. Bring along your transcript to that meeting to confirm that you're on track. You might want to focus on which courses in your major will provide credits when you transfer. And note that if the committee at your choice four-year college chooses not to transfer credits for a particular course you've taken—and for which you believe you should get credit—don't give up. You may be able to protest the decision by appealing to the head of the degree program in which you are enrolling.

QUESTIONS FOR YOUR PREADMISSIONS ADVISOR

- What is the minimum grade you need to receive transfer credit for the class?
- Which courses will transfer as credit in your major and which as electives?
- Do your grades transfer (your GPA) or just the course credit?
- Will the college accept your scores on standardized tests such as the CLEP?
- Is there a statute of limitations on transfer credits? Many colleges will not accept credit for classes taken more than seven years prior to transfer.
- Will you get credit for doing well on placement tests? How about credits earned in the military?
- Will you be required to take placement tests again even though you've already completed your remedial classes? Are there any other exams you need to take such as the SAT or TOEFL?

Visit the Campus

Meeting the representatives from four-year colleges and talking to their school advisors is important, but once you've narrowed your choices of target schools, it's important that you visit the campus yourself and get a sense of the school in its actual setting. Only by spending time there can you garner a feel for the students at the college, the physical layout of the campus, a realistic guess at the travel time to get there, and all sorts of other nonquantifiable features of the school.

DIFFICULT AND EASY TRANSFERS

Thus far, we've focused on how to transfer once you've completed your course work and been awarded your community college degree. But suppose you want to transfer before you've received your AA or AS degree? Our advice: don't.

When to Transfer

Transferring before graduating puts you in jeopardy of losing credits, which, in turn, translates into extra time and money. Many states mandate that their four-year public colleges accept all your credits upon completion of the AA or AS degree, but these schools can choose which credits to accept if you transfer before completion of your two-year course work. So if you're determined to transfer early, be aware you risk losing credits for classes you've taken.

Nevertheless, if you decide you must transfer early, there are some things you can do to improve your chance of gaining acceptance and credits. For example, four-year colleges tend to be favorably disposed to community college honors courses so try to take these classes if you can. And if you've received any awards such as the dean's list or are a member of an academic honor society such as Phi Theta Kappa, your application will be that much more appealing to a four-year college (plus you'll enhance your chance to receive a scholarship).

Maintain a Folder of Information

Over the years, you'll be collecting lots of information about transferring. Don't imagine you can keep all of it in your head. Keep a folder with the relevant data organized into sections: perhaps one devoted to money matters—scholarship possibilities and the like; another listing how credits will be accepted by various colleges; another showing which if any schools have articulation agreements with your school in your area of study; one keeping useful handouts you've collected at transfer fairs and workshops along with transfer newsletters your college has produced; another reviewing conversations you've had with advisors at your own college and, later, at your target four-year school; and still another with a current transcript. There will likely be other sections you'll want to include as well. Later, when it comes time to make some decisions, you'll be pleased you have all this useful information in one place.

AND REMEMBER...

Your decision to continue your education after community college reflects the seriousness with which you approach your education and career. But the process involves many small steps and institutional details, and the burden to be on top of it all is primarily on you. The time to start planning your transfer to a four-year college begins as soon as you enroll in community college, and this responsibility is ongoing. Get the information you need, and be organized and persistent, and your transition will be smooth and efficient.

Master key strategies of the job search—networking, résumé writing, and excelling at your interview— and you'll be on your way to translating your college experience into the job you desire.

The Real World: Landing the First Job of Your New Career

ONE GLORIOUS MORNING you wake up to find you're about to complete your final college courses before graduation. Perhaps, as discussed in the previous chapter, you'll be transferring to a four-year school and preparing for additional education. On the other hand, you might intend to begin work in the career for which you studied these past years. You'll need to approach the job search with the same care and determination you applied to your courses. And you'll need to master a set of new skills that includes résumé writing, networking, and successful interviewing to land that desirable job. In this chapter, we'll review these key marketing elements you'll need to promote yourself in the workplace.

COMMUNICATING YOUR CREDENTIALS

If your aim in community college was to use your degree or certificate to help get you started in a related career, you'll want to begin this job search as you near graduation. Among the first items on your to-do list is to compose the documents that will feature your credentials.

Creating Your First Résumé

A résumé is a summary of your schooling, experience, and qualifications. You'll need to send your prospective employer a résumé or bring one with you to the job interview.

WHO WOULD'VE THOUGHT?

You have heard the expression "First impressions are lasting impressions." Well, your résumé is the first meeting between you and a prospective employer, and it's vital that you make a good first impression.[1]

If this is your first venture into the workplace, you might be wondering, "What can I put on my résumé? I haven't accomplished anything yet." And even if you have been working these past years, you might be entering a new career with little or no background in the field worth mentioning. Think again. You have a lot more experience than you might suppose. Presenting yourself in a favorable light is the challenge of good résumé construction.

Because the résumé is so important in helping attain a desired job, some companies charge high fees to prepare a résumé for you. However, if you understand what key elements belong in a résumé and how to organize them, you should be able to compose an effective résumé on your own. As you compose this résumé, remember that its central purpose is not to get you a job, but to help you get a job interview.

DIGGING DEEPER

A well-written "classical" résumé can open many doors for you in traditional industries. However, when applying for a job with a Web or tech-savvy company, you may want to consider a résumé that links to a relevant Web site, a project you've created, or your own Web site or blog.

Choosing a Résumé Style

Résumés can be classified into three main types. The *chronological résumé* lists your employment and education history through time; it is also, more accurately, called a *reverse chronological résumé* because the first item in the list is your most recent information, followed by the next most recent, and on backward. A *functional* or *skills résumé* highlights the skills and accomplishments you've acquired through the course of your education and work career. Your most important ability is noted first, followed by the second most important, and so on in this fashion. A *hybrid* or *combination résumé,* as the name implies, combines the résumé types above. In general, a hybrid résumé is best.

As a recent college graduate, in particular, you should favor a functional or hybrid résumé so that you can underscore your abilities rather than your work experience (which, at this point, might be minimal). If you've had jobs during your college years, you'll be able to note your work responsibilities and accomplishments as well.

As you work on your résumé, get needed help from some of the many books and Web sites devoted to résumé writing. With diligence and care, you can produce an excellent résumé on your own—and save the money for an interview suit.

HELPFUL WEB SITES FOR YOUR FIRST RÉSUMÉ

http://www.eresumes.com
>   This site includes sample résumés, job-specific résumés, and information on e-portfolios.

http://www.monsterguide.net/how-to-write-a-resume.shtml
>   Monster Guide details each part of the résumé.

http://www.rogers-resume-help-center.com/10-top-resume-writing-tips.html
>   This site contains a good step-by-step review of the résumé-writing process, but be wary of the heavy-handed sales pitch.

http://www.wikihow.com/Make-a-Resume
>   WikiHow provides steps for creating a résumé and includes a video.

http://www.diversityinc.com/public/3551.cfm
>   DiversityInc includes a terrific top ten résumé blunders list—a must-see.

http://www.soyouwanna.com/site/syws/resume/resume.html
This site will walk you through the résumé-writing process and give you a couple of smiles along the way.

http://www.soyouwanna.com/site/syws/resume/sampleresume.pdf
This is a good sample résumé.

http://www.trincoll.edu/depts/career/guides/resume.shtml
This site offers an excellent step-by-step approach and includes a sample résumé as well as a list of action words to use when creating your own.

http://www.provenresumes.com
This is the site of a résumé-writing service, but it also includes free résumé-writing strategies and a rate-your-résumé quiz.

http://www.collegegrad.com/resumes
This site provides sample entry-level résumés, which are especially useful for new college graduates.

Basic Elements of a Résumé

Your research will uncover a variety of résumé styles, but the basic elements of a résumé will be the same throughout. These key features are:

- Your name and contact information clearly stated at the top, including address, e-mail address, and phone details. If you have an e-mail address such as hotfunkymamma@gmail.com, now is the time to create a new one. You can keep your informal e-mail address for your friends, but choose something more professional for prospective employers.
- Your degree. List your expected graduation date.
- Your list of objectives. Not all résumés include objectives, but it may be helpful to your potential employers if you note your career aims and the sort of work you're looking for to further your career goals.
- Previous jobs that contain significant accomplishments or responsibilities. Mention also any awards, honors, or extracurricular activities that speak to your qualifications for the job, as well as language, computer, or other relevant proficiencies.
- References. Although not mandatory, you might include the names of two references.

SAMPLE RÉSUMÉ

The following is an example of a hybrid résumé.

Lisette P. Rostern

35 East Burgos Street, Chicago, IL 60641 (773) 555-1234, LRostern@gmail.com

Summary Experience: Organization oriented with strong communication and people skills. Strong familiarity with computer information systems, expense reports, travel and event planning, video setup, and teleconferencing.

Computer Skills: Microsoft Word, Microsoft Excel, Adobe Photoshop, Lotus Notes

EXPERIENCE:

Administrative

Administrative Assistant, June 2007– present
Williams Communications, Indianapolis, IN
- Provide administrative support to the Communications Director of a large video production company.
- Schedule all conferences, teleconferences, and video shoots.
- Create and oversee all video inventory reports.
- Establish travel expenditure reporting systems.

Information Systems

Administrative Assistant, September 2001–2005
Billinsly & Co., New York, NY
- Managed small, independently owned equities office.
- Initiated computer system to track all travel and expenses of staff of twelve.
- Launched speaker series of equity brokers.

Web Manager, September 1999–2000
Malcolm X High School, Chicago, IL
- Designed, set up, and maintained class Web site.
- Provided support for students with technical problems or questions about the site.

EDUCATION:

Truman College, Chicago, IL, June 2009
AS in Business Administration with a Marketing minor, GPA 3.7

Additional Skills And Interests:
- Moderate fluency in Spanish.
- Broad knowledge of photography and videography.
- Extensive travel throughout the United States and Europe.

- Do not lie. Don't even exaggerate. But do present your experience and achievements in the most positive light.
- And tailor your résumé to the job you're seeking. Word processing programs make it easy to adapt your résumé to fit each job for which you're applying.

Presentation Matters

Your résumé should be no more than one to two pages. It should be easy to read, concise, and clear. Use a medium-sized font, and print on a fairly heavyweight white or ivory bond paper. This is not the time to exhibit your cool neon stationary. Do not use erasable paper. Make sure you have a copy of your résumé on a computer, as you will want to submit both a hard copy and an electronic version, and retain a copy for yourself as well. Proofread *very* carefully. Grammatical, spelling, and typing errors leave a negative impression, no matter how convincing your résumé is otherwise. (It's a good idea to have another person read over your résumé; we're too involved in the content of our work and apt to miss even obvious errors.)

The Cover Letter

When applying for a job, you can't just shove your résumé in an envelope and drop it in the mail. Your résumé needs to be accompanied by a well-written, targeted cover letter.

Cover letters should be brief and to the point. Some job seekers think they can help themselves stand out from the crowd by writing unorthodox or even bizarre cover letters. Rarely does this have the desired effect. In most cases, it's a turnoff that will undermine your application.

As with your résumé, it's a good idea to create a strong standard cover letter and then adjust the letter to target the specifics of the job for which you are applying.

As you can see, this cover letter is short and to the point. First, directly address the person doing the hiring if possible. Then introduce yourself and state the job for which you are applying. Also mention that you're enclosing your résumé. It's also helpful to note, as this letter does, how you learned of the job (from a newspaper

SAMPLE COVER LETTER

12345 Whitehall Road
Creighton, OH 01010
May 2, 2009

Addy's Ad Company
Dalton, OH

Dear Mr. Allred,

My name is Pamela Lee, and I will be graduating from Hopewell Community College in June with an AAS in Graphic Design. I am enclosing my résumé in response to your advertisement for a management associate in the March 25th edition of the Daily Ledger. I have been working as a graphic artist intern for the past three years at Nicholas Advertising Agency and feel I have all of the designer qualifications you seek.

I can be reached during the day on my cell phone at 617-555-1212 or by e-mail at pamlee@gmail.com. I would very much like an opportunity to sit down with you and discuss the opportunity to work at your agency.

Thank you for your time and attention. I look forward to hearing from you.

Sincerely,

Pamela Lee

---

advertisement, an online posting, at your college employment service, and so on).

The same presentation guidelines for résumés apply to cover letters: use white or ivory non-erasable paper and a medium-sized font. Be assured that, though it might seem a formality and barely examined by your potential employer, your cover letter is essential to the job search process. Your prospective employers may throw the cover letter away, but if it isn't enclosed, your résumé is likely to be tossed as well.

WEB SITES TO HELP YOU CREATE A COVER LETTER

Your computer's word processing program and Web browser can help you compose a suitable cover letter. Microsoft Word, for example, offers cover letter templates you can modify as needed. But be judicious; not every sample cover letter will work for you on every occasion. Many of these templates are too pushy, others too long and chatty, and others too vague. The following are sites that—provided you're selective and careful—can help you find the right tone and content for your cover letter.

http://www.quintcareers.com/cover_letter_samples.html
    Quintessential Careers offers a broad range of cover letters for every point in your career, whether you're applying for an internship, you've just graduated from college, or you're changing jobs.
http://www.quintcareers.com/cover_letter_checklist.html
    This site also offers a good checklist of important features of the cover letter.
http://docs.google.com/View?docid=dd8nn97m_39skpwscj&hl=en_US&pageview=1&hgd=1
    This is a cover letter template ready to be filled in.
http://jobsearch.about.com/od/coverlettersamples/a/covertemplate.htm
    This site from About.com explains the structure of the cover letter.
http://jobsearch.about.com/od/coverlettersamples/a/emailcover.htm
    About.com also offers guidance on writing e-mail cover letters.

FROM THE AUTHORS' FILES

As the chairperson of an academic department and a former executive at a media company, I have seen a lot of résumés and cover letters. The advice we have given here is spot-on and should be followed unfailingly. Résumés that arrive messy and poorly written with smudges and/or typos rarely make it through the hiring committee. Sloppy cover letters also invariably condemn the résumé to the rejection file. On the other hand, I recall a pristine and articulate résumé and cover letter that I received from someone who had graduated from my department five years earlier and had transferred to a four-year school. That former student has now been working with us for two years, proving that a well-done résumé and cover letter, along with networking, make an almost unbeatable combination. *DG*

NETWORKING

We've discussed the résumé and cover letter you submit in response to a print advertisement or an online job notice. But your response can also be a follow-up to an employment opportunity that comes to your attention through other, personal channels—your network.

Networking is the art of building alliances. Networking is not about calling everyone you've ever met and asking them for a job. It is about creating and nurturing relationships long before you begin looking for a job. There's nothing unseemly or scheming about networking; we do it all the time. Think back to when you were introduced to the manager at your work–study assignment. Do you remember some of the people you met when you attended that professional organization meeting? How about the people you talk with at your house of worship? Or those people involved in your block's development program? Or even that individual with whom you had an interesting conversation at the doctor's office or a friend's party? We are constantly meeting people and forging relationships. This is networking. The time to call on that network is now, when you are looking for work.

Why are these relationships so important to our job search? Because, as often noted, so many available jobs are never advertised! Networking is how you find and succeed at these employment opportunities. In hiring new employees, employers prefer to rely on recommendations from people who already work for them or from people they know personally. These connections are your first references.

But networking, like all else in the job searching, takes work to make it work. Here are some ways to develop your network:

- Attend job fairs. Most colleges will sponsor at least one such fair a year. Here you'll get to mingle with potential employers and hand them your résumé, allowing them to connect a face and personality to that piece of paper.
- Keep in touch with people you've met in your various jobs. Whether it was a summer internship or work at the supermarket, let these individuals know that you are graduating with a degree in your chosen field, and ask them to inform you of possible job opportunities.
- After graduation, join your college's alumni association. This is an opportunity to meet periodically with people who have potential connections in your field of interest and will be happy to lend a hand to fellow alumni. Alumni associations also offer workshops in résumé writing and interviewing and can be a terrific resource for honest feedback and helpful tips on improving your job search.
- Follow up on all those connections we noted above—organizations, religious institutions, alumni, family, friends, and friends of friends. Let them know you're in the job market. You'll be surprised by the number of people who—and which people will—provide you with promising leads.

WHO WOULD'VE THOUGHT?

According to CareerXroads's 2007 Annual Source of Hire Survey, 34 percent of new hires brought in from outside an organization were a result of employee referrals.[2]

PREPARING FOR YOUR JOB INTERVIEW

Don't expect your résumé or your network of relationships to get you a job all by themselves. It's not likely that someone will read your résumé or have a fifteen-minute chat with you at a professional organization and immediately call to ask you to begin work the next Monday. Your network increases the addresses to which you distribute your résumé, and your résumé and cover letter are your calling cards. Together they are designed to get you a job interview. And it's at the interview that you will make the impression that will result in a job offer.

To get ready for an interview, you need to do some careful preparation.

Research the Company

In preparing for the interview, you'll want to find out as much as possible about the company or organization to which you're applying. Through friends, employees, and Web sites, learn as much as you can about the company's philosophy, sales, goals, employer–employee relationships, and so on. Your interviewers are sure to ask you why you want to work at their company, and you will impress them with an informed answer that demonstrates a genuine familiarity with the organization.

Toward the end of the interview, you're sure to be asked if you have any questions. Again, prior research will help you devise a targeted, intelligent question or two. For help with forming more general questions, check out About.com's "Interview Questions and Answers" page at http://jobsearch.about.com/od/interviewquestionsanswers/a/interviewquest2.htm.

Prepare Yourself and Your Online Presence

Be aware that while you're researching the company in preparation for your interview, the company might be researching you. If you have a MySpace page or a Facebook page with provocative pictures of your wild parties—or even odd, unprofessional photos—consider removing them. Just as you switched from the funky e-mail address to a more professional one, so too you might want to edit your Internet presence as well as your voice mail message (the sexy breathing or blaring music in the background won't help establish your image as a serious professional).

In addition to preparing for the interview by researching the company and editing your online personae, you need to be familiar with the types of questions typically asked in interviews. You don't want to memorize your response, but you also don't want to appear completely stumped by these questions, fumbling for answers.

TYPICAL INTERVIEW QUESTIONS

- Tell me about yourself. (Be careful not to go on too long with your answer.)
- What do you know about our company? (You should know enough, so do the research.)
- Why should we hire you? (Highlight your relevant abilities.)
- What can you do for us that someone else can't? (You bring distinctive talents and eagerness for this job.)
- What do you look for in a job? (You want to learn, and you welcome responsibility.)
- How does this assignment fit into your overall career plan? (Mention your career goals, and, if possible, note how you can meet those goals at this company.)
- Do you work well with others? (Recount specific examples of how you were an effective leader and worked well with others. Employers are looking for team players who work well collaboratively.)
- How would your colleagues describe you? (Be honest, but of course draw attention to the positive.)
- What do you think of your present or past boss? (Don't be negative; you don't want to appear as a complainer.)
- What were the most significant accomplishments in your career so far? (Be prepared with a few examples.)
- Can you work well under deadlines or pressure? (Of course you can.)
- What salary do you expect if offered the position? (Make sure you know what the going rate for someone with your experience and job responsibility.)
- Why do you want to work for us? (Have a ready response.)
- Do you have your reference list with you? (Have a list prepared, but don't offer it unless you're asked for it.)

The following are a few Web sites that review standard interview questions:

http://www.wisebread.com/how-to-answer-23-of-the-most-common-interview-questions

Wise Bread provides a guide for answering typical interview questions and counsels you in thinking about the answers.

http://www.careercc.com/interv3.shtml
> Career Consulting Corner offers a good overview of tips to follow
> when interviewing.

THE JOB INTERVIEW

You've written your résumé, networked, landed a job interview, and prepared for your job interview. Great! But you still aren't ready for your first paycheck. You still need to show up at the interview and make the impression that will secure you the job offer. Here are several things to remember as you prepare for this important meeting.

"Dress For Success" Is Not a Cliché

Is it unfair for people to judge people on what they wear? Perhaps. But everyone does. And they will at your job interview. So make sure you show up with an appropriate interview outfit.

Your clothes needn't be expensive, but they should be clean, neat, and professional looking. If you're a male and don't own a suit, this might be the right time to purchase one. Even if you might not be required to wear a suit once hired, wearing one at the interview signals that you take the job seriously.

If you're a female and unsure of what to wear, it's always better to err on the side of conservative—"dressy" rather than casual. Suits, dresses, or coordinated jackets and skirts are the norm for interviews. Limit your jewelry, and avoid long earrings and long nail extensions.

Male or female, keep perfume and cologne to a minimum. In addition, don't have anything in your mouth such as gum or mints, and make sure not to smell of tobacco or alcohol.

The Big Day

There will be many things on your mind on the day of the interview. But you can help your cause if you have prepared an "interview toolbox," the essential items to bring with you to the interview.

Your Résumé

Your interviewer will probably have a copy of your résumé waiting on his or her desk. But bring an updated copy with you just in case.

Pad and Pencil or Pen

Bring a pad of paper and a writing instrument to write comments, impressions, questions, or answers. You may want to jot down a resource or Web site or make note of a next meeting. Moreover, you might be asked to provide additional information and don't want later to forget what it was. Write it down.

A Portfolio of Your Work

Bring along a portfolio of your work if you have one. This can be especially useful in jobs such as digital arts, advertising, and marketing. Your portfolio will showcase the high caliber of your work.

References

If you have chosen not to include your references on your résumé, have those names and contact numbers prepared on a single sheet of paper.

Cell Phone

This is one day you don't want to forget your cell phone. If you're delayed in traffic or on the train, you'll want to get in touch with your interviewer and explain your lateness. Conversely, you want your interviewer to get in touch if he or she had to change plans. And, of course, you also want the interviewer to have that number when he or she calls you to offer you the job. But please remember to shut off the phone before you begin the interview.

Interviewer Contact and Location

So many people forget to bring the name of the person who will interview them and have to ask the receptionist. Know whom you'll be talking with and in which office the interviewer works.

In addition to this "toolbox," there are other things to consider as you ready yourself for the interview.

Show Up on Time

Few things give as immediate and as negative an impression as showing up late for an interview. Try to arrive at the correct location at least a half hour before the scheduled interview time. If you come early enough, you can find a café or diner, have a cup of tea or coffee, collect your thoughts, and then make your way to the interview without rushing to your destination.

Attitude

Throughout your interview, you need to present yourself as confident and positive. A defeatist attitude might well cost you the job. But appreciate the difference between appearing self-assured and appearing arrogant.

Remain upbeat and friendly even if you think you haven't answered a question fully. As the interview progresses, you and your interviewer will gain a comfort level with each other, and it might be your sociable demeanor that decides the job offer in your favor.

What Not to Do

And now for a few things to avoid at your interview.

- Don't mumble. Communicating clearly is essential and goes a long way toward having a successful interview.
- Don't use inappropriate language. This isn't the time to lapse into slang or off-color language—even if you think you've established a casual friendliness with your interviewer.
- Don't bad mouth your previous employer. No matter how you feel about him or her, no matter how horrible he or she was, now is not the time to express your anger. If asked why you left your last position, construct an answer that keeps your negative feelings to yourself.
- Don't talk about personal issues. Avoid details about your private life that can raise negative concerns or have no relevance to the position, such as political and religious beliefs or the sordid particulars of your recent breakup.

After the Interview

Within twenty-four hours after the interview, send a thank you note to your interviewer. Less than 5 percent of job applicants do this; yet, studies show that thank you notes can be extremely helpful in securing a job offer.[3]

WHO WOULD'VE THOUGHT?

A survey by CareerBuilders.com reports that nearly 15 percent of hiring managers would reject a job candidate who neglected to send a thank you letter after the interview.[4]

A thank you note gives you one more opportunity to sell yourself to your prospective employer. In this note, in addition to thanking the interviewer for his or her time and consideration, you can briefly reiterate your skills, background, and interest in the job and perhaps refer to something important you might have forgotten during the interview. A thank you note also demonstrates that you're courteous and understand the protocol of the professional world. For samples of thank you notes visit http://www.quintcareers.com/sample_thank-you_letters.html.

AND REMEMBER...

You've studied long and hard these past years. You've mastered new skills and readied yourself for a new career. Now it's time to get out there and begin that journey. But don't expect the path to be easy. Be prepared for dozens of unanswered résumés. Be prepared for numerous interviews. But persist and maintain a positive attitude, and that job and flourishing career is sure to come your way.

As you prepare to move on to the next chapter of your life, continued education at a four-year college or a job in your chosen field, confirm that you've met all your school's requirements—academic, administrative, and financial—and then reward yourself with a well-deserved graduation ceremony.

The Last Lap: Commencement and Beyond

SO IT'S FINALLY HERE, and you can hardly believe it. The proverbial "light at the end of the tunnel" is no longer only a light but a full-fledged blinding beam. You've marked commencement day on your calendar. And it's arriving soon.

But busy as you are with your final semester's schoolwork and other commitments to your work and family, you might neglect those last steps you need to take to graduate.

REQUIREMENTS FOR GRADUATION

Throughout your college years, you've been working with a counselor or academic advisor in choosing courses to satisfy the requirements of your academic program. However, to be eligible for graduation, there are other requirements to be met in addition to the completion of these designated courses.

The Fundamentals

These requirements vary from school to school, but the following are several that are shared by nearly all.

Degree Audit

A *degree audit,* or *academic audit,* is a computer-generated analysis that compares the college courses you have completed with the requirements of the degree. Many colleges will ask you to obtain an official audit, though some schools allow you to access this audit on your own (as you might have been doing all along). Usually you can connect to the online college system to determine whether you have the sufficient and correct credits to graduate. (You may know the degree audit by the name of the software program that runs it: DegreeWorks, Degree Solutions, and Degree Audit Report [DAR] are among the more widespread programs.) Some schools will not permit you to graduate unless your degree audit is signed by your academic advisor and submitted to the registrar's office.

Minimum Credit Hours

Generally, community colleges require a minimum of sixty successfully completed credits for you to be eligible for an associate's degree. Students sometimes worry so much about completing the courses in their major that they forget to pay attention to other courses and electives they must complete to graduate. Make sure to keep track of all your courses, so you don't come up short at the last minute.

Credits in Residency

Most schools require that you complete a minimum number of credits at their school before they grant you a degree. This is understandable; the college doesn't want to issue a degree to someone who completed only one course at the school! If you've attended the same community college throughout, this isn't of concern to you. But if you've transferred from another two-year or a four-year college, make certain that you've completed the requisite number of credits at your current school. This minimum can be stipulated as a percentage of credits (for example, 25 percent of the required credits needed for graduation) or as a designated number of credits (for example, twenty credits or more). Ideally, you found out about this policy as soon as you transferred to your current school or as soon as possible thereafter.

Good Standing

To graduate, you must be considered a student in good standing. The prevailing academic definition of good standing is having achieved a minimum of a 2.0 GPA. (We assume you've been calculating your GPA regularly. See Chapter 12 for a review.) Some schools might allow you to graduate with a slightly lower average and extenuating circumstances, but many are rigid about the C or better GPA. The moral? Make sure your GPA is above the cutoff before applying to graduate.

Fulfillment of Financial Obligations to the College

Remember that book you borrowed from the library three semesters ago? The one you forgot to return on time? You may have forgotten, but the college hasn't! You will not be permitted to graduate unless you've paid off all the fees you owe to the school. These debts can run the gamut from unpaid parking tickets to late returns of DVDs to laboratory fees and costs for art supplies. Don't let an outstanding bill for a test tube impede your future.

WHO WOULD'VE THOUGHT?

Yes, the paying of fees goes on until the end of your college days (and beyond, if you join the alumni association). When you file your application for graduation, you may also be required to cover the cost of your cap and gown and diploma. Many schools include this fee whether or not you participate in the formal commencement exercises.

Application to Graduate

Your college isn't keeping tabs on when you plan to graduate. You have to let it know by filing a letter of intent. The form is straightforward, but you do need to be aware of the deadline for filing. Deadlines vary widely from school to school; some expect the application as early as after the first three weeks of your graduating term, and others allow you up to three weeks before graduation day. Check your school's Web site to find out when this document must be submitted.

GRADUATION CHECKLIST

Here is a general checklist to review before graduation. Make sure to check with your college for its own additional requirements.

- *Do a degree audit.* Obtain or conduct the audit either on your own or with your academic advisor.
- *Have your transcript evaluated.* If you have credit from a previous school or institution that needs to be evaluated for your program, confirm that the admissions, registration, and records offices have received your official transcripts before you submit your graduation application.
- *See your academic advisor.* Any problems or inconsistencies may be cleared up at this time.
- *Meet all financial obligations.* Make sure you have no outstanding financial obligations to the school.
- *Apply for graduation.* Make sure to note deadlines.
- *Verify your name.* Notify the school of any name changes to be sure your records and diploma reflect your correct name.
- *Provide a best address for future contact.*
- *Order your cap and gown.*
- *Stop by the bookstore.* Ask about dates for book buybacks; it's easier to sell your books while you're still on campus.
- *Deal with your education loans.* Inform your lender/holder that you've graduated, and, if appropriate, update your address and phone number.

Graduation Requirements: The Add-Ons

In addition to the credit and GPA requirements for graduation, many colleges also stipulate that you take assessment tests. You might be groaning at the thought of yet another exam and understandably so. Well, at least only one of these tests can have an impact on your graduation.

Skills Assessments

Skills assessments are exams that test specific abilities. Passage of this exam is required for graduation. For example, City University of New York (CUNY) students must pass the CUNY Proficiency Exam (CPE) in writing and critical thinking. This three-hour exam consists of an analytical reading and writing component as well as a section on analyzing and integrating material from texts and graphs. In Florida, all community college students must take the five-hour College-Level Academic Skills Test (CLAST), which consists of four subtests in essay writing, English language skills (ELS), reading, and mathematics.

University Assessments

The other type of assessment exam is designed to assess the school, *not* you, the student. You may be required to take this exam to graduate, but you need not pass the exam to graduate. For example, California requires both the Collegiate Assessment of Academic Proficiency (CAAP) and the California Critical Thinking Skills Test (CCTST). The CAAP is a forty-five-minute assessment session conducted in a group setting. The CCTST is a thirty-four-question assessment that evaluates your ability to think logically and reason clearly. You cannot study for this test, and your results are immaterial to your graduation. The aim of these tests is to serve as a tool for the college to better evaluate how well it is doing in preparing its students for their careers and further education.

Even More Specific Graduation Requirements

The requirements discussed above are standard, shared by probably 90 percent of community colleges. In addition, however, many states and colleges have their own unique requirements.

Portfolios

Some community colleges now require students to submit a select compilation of their college work. This portfolio—or *e-portfolio,* as it is called when presented in electronic form—can include output from over your entire college career or just over the most recent semesters.

You should find out as soon as possible if a portfolio is a requirement for graduation and what is expected in this collection.

Research Paper

Some schools require the submission of a research paper for graduation. No doubt you've written a few research papers and have one ready, but you'll want to make sure the paper you submit meets the college's standards for research, organization, and writing.

Capstone Courses

Capstone courses are required primarily in curricula geared toward employment upon graduation or as part of a general education program. These classes are designed to pull together the key learning objectives of your course of study. You're expected to take your capstone class in your last semester in college.

Special Courses

Some states expect their students to enroll in a specific class before graduation.

The state of Illinois, for example, requires community college students to take a political science course covering the American national government or to pass an exam prepared by the state on the Illinois constitution and the United States Constitution. Many of the community colleges in California comply with the state's directive about information competency and require a class in library studies or another course that reinforces information competency. Because you don't want any last-minute surprises, find out if your college, too, has a special course requirement.

 DIGGING DEEPER

Students at Northwest State Community College in Archbold, Ohio, are required to take at least one online course to graduate.[1]

Occupational Assessment

If you are graduating with a degree designed to facilitate your entry into the workforce, you may be asked to have an occupational assessment. This may be an exam created by an accrediting organization or by your department. Or the occupational assessment might entail a review of a product or project you've completed. For example, if you're looking to enter the television field as a cameraperson or film editor, you may be asked to submit a video or reel of your best works.

COMMENCEMENT

You're done. You've passed all your finals in your final semester. You've paid the parking ticket and even sold half your textbooks back to the bookstore. Your advisor has cleared you to graduate. Get ready to celebrate. Buy yourself that item you've been eyeing; you've earned it. And get ready for commencement.

WHO WOULD'VE THOUGHT?

You've done something really special by getting this college degree. According to the Family Care Foundation, if we reduced the world's population to a village of precisely one hundred people, with all existing human ratios remaining the same, the demographics would look something like this: sixty-seven would be unable to read, only seven would have access to the Internet, and *one* would be a college graduate.[2]

The commencement ceremony is where academic degrees are conferred and where you'll receive that piece of paper for which you've worked so hard. The name of this concluding celebration has an interesting double meaning. Although the ceremony marks the end of your time at the college, to *commence* means to begin, and, indeed, graduation is also the beginning of the next chapter of your life.

You might be a bit cynical about commencement exercises. In many high schools, anyone who managed to attend school for four years automatically graduates (and these days, children have major commencement events for completing kindergarten). But you ought not to be so dismissive of this forthcoming event. It's important that you do make a big deal about this day. The commencement is a tribute to your achievement. It's a special day you won't forget.

FROM THE AUTHORS' FILES

Commencement never fails to move me. The excitement of the students I have taught or mentored, the pride on their faces as well as those of their parents and family, the music, the ceremonial dress—this is, indeed, a memorable day. It is now many years after the receipt of my doctorate degree and commencement, and I remember every moment of it. So if you are questioning whether to attend, weighing the cost of the gown and the babysitter, debate no further. It really is the first day of the rest of your life, and you should be there to cherish it. The memory of the day that honored your accomplishment will be a treasure you will own forever. *DG*

Commencement exercises differ from college to college, so consider the following few issues as you prepare for the event.

Commencement Calendar

Many—perhaps most—community colleges conduct only one commencement ceremony a year, usually in the spring. But because schools work on a semester, tri-semester, or quarter semester schedule, you might complete your course work at the end of the summer or in January and have to wait until the end of spring for your commencement. Despite the delay and the postponed excitement, we strongly urge that you don't lose your enthusiasm for your graduation ceremony.

DIGGING DEEPER

If you have a disability, your college will arrange assistance so that you can participate in your commencement. Similarly, if you have a guest attending who requires special accommodation, notify your school. This is a major event for the college as well, and the school's Office of Student Affairs will see to it that your special needs and those of your guests are met.

Other Things to Consider

There are details other than the date to deal with in planning for this memorable occasion. The following are a few.

Cap and Gown

As mentioned above, the charge for caps and gowns is sometimes included in the application for graduation fee. However, some schools have the gown company contact you directly. Make sure to find out what procedure your school follows. You don't want to show up on this big day without the ceremonial regalia! The tassel's worth the hassle!

Commencement Tickets and Knowing Where to Go

You will probably be allotted a limited number of tickets to the graduation ceremony; however, events held outdoors usually allow for more guests. Tickets are given away quickly, so a delay in picking up yours will leave you with fewer to distribute to your friends and family.

Colleges prefer to hold their commencements outdoors even in poor weather so that they can accommodate a larger number of guests. But check your college Web site to learn of a contingency plan in case the school decides to move the commencement indoors.

Photographer

This is an event in your life worth documenting. You might have a friend or someone in your family bring along a still camera or video camera, or perhaps you prefer to hire your own film crew. Go right ahead. But be aware that your college also arranges for a professional photographer to capture that glorious moment when you receive your diploma on stage. Find out if these photos are available for purchase.

Diplomas

Don't be surprised if instead of the real diploma, you're handed a blank cover. In many instances, the college has not yet received all student grades before commencement. Diplomas are often mailed four to six weeks after final certification by the college.

After Graduation

Take a break. Your next life experience will begin soon enough. In the meantime, take the moment, days, and weeks to relax and savor your achievement

AND REMEMBER . . .

During the graduation ceremony, you'll hear speakers remind you to relish your memories of your college years. They will exhort you to value your education and perhaps quote Benjamin Franklin's insight that "an investment in knowledge always pays the best interest." No doubt you'll be called upon to make the world a better place than you found it. Guess what? All of it is true. This day can be both a celebration and a turning point in your life. So don't live down the expectations. Get out there and do something remarkable. And congratulations!

APPENDIX A:

Community College Speak:
Terms You Need to Know

AA: Abbreviation for an "associate of arts" degree, one of the degrees offered at community colleges.

AAS: Abbreviation for an "associate of applied science" degree, one of the degrees offered at community colleges.

AS: Abbreviation for an "associates of science" degree, one of the degrees offered at community colleges.

ACT: Test that measures a student's aptitude in English, mathematics, reading, science reasoning, and writing.

Academic Advisor: Faculty member or college staff who aids students with course selection and development of an academic plan.

Academic Calendar: Calendar that provides key dates and deadlines—by semester—for an academic year, including add/drop deadlines, registration dates, mid-term and final exam periods, school holidays, and more.

Academic Probation: Warning to the student that his or her academic progress is unsatisfactory.

Academic Standing: Scholastic standing of a student based on his or her grade point average (GPA).

Academic Support Centers: Place at a college that provides no-cost instructional services to students to assist them in achieving better academic success, generally focusing on writing and math.

Accreditation: Assessment of a college or academic program by one or more outside organizations. Accreditation organizations certify that an institution or program is following defined guidelines and policies.

Adjunct Faculty: Part-time instructors that colleges hire to teach classes.

Admission: Process of filling out forms, filing documents, and taking tests prior to actual registration.

Application: One-time process to enroll in a college as a student.

Articulation Agreement: Arrangement between colleges that facilitates the transfer of credits from one school to the other by agreeing that certain courses offered at one school are the equivalent to those offered at the other.

BA: Abbreviation for a "bachelor of arts," a degree that can be earned at four-year colleges.

BS: Abbreviation for a "bachelor of science," a degree that can be earned at four-year colleges.

Blackboard: Software application commonly referred to as a Course Management System, which allows students to access online course content.

Blue Book: Small, historically blue-covered booklets with ruled notebook paper. Used for short-answer and essay exams, these booklets are now available in a variety of colored covers.

Certificate Program: Group of related courses designed to provide expertise in a particular field. Typically completed in about one year when the student is enrolled full-time, a program may take longer if prerequisites are required.

Class Schedule: List of classes that a student is enrolled in during a term, including course names and sections, instructor, meeting days, meeting times, and location.

Class Standing: Student's official year in school based on the number of college credits completed.

Commencement: Graduation exercises at which academic degrees are conferred to students.

Convocation: College-wide gatherings, typically held at the beginning of a term, in which the top administrators discuss the accomplishments of the institution, welcome new students, and sometimes present awards to top-performing students.

Core Classes: Required classes for all students in a major program.

Corequisite: Course that must be taken at the same time as another course.

Course: Organized class on specific subject matter in which instruction is offered within a given period of time and for which one usually receives credit toward graduation or certification.

Course Catalogue: Official booklet of a college that details critical information about admissions and academic requirements, majors and minors, and courses of study.

Course Description: Summary containing important information about the nature and goals of a course as well as required pre-requisites. Typically found in the course catalogue (and sometimes on the course syllabus).

Course Load: Number of credit hours for which a student is enrolled in a given term. These typically differ for part-time status and full-time students. For example, in a semester system, a full-time course load is generally twelve or more credit hours.

Course Number: Cataloging system that contains a series of letters and numbers to designate a course in a department.

Credit Hour: Unit of measurement that determines the amount of class time required each week of a term. In a typical semester system, a 3-hour class requires classes to meet in three 1-hour sessions, two 1.5-hour sessions, or one 3-hour session.

Curriculum: Body of courses required for a certificate, degree, or diploma, or constituting a major field of study.

Dean: Upper-level administrative officer of a division, college, or school, such as Dean of Academic Affairs.

Debar: To preclude a student from attending class due to lack of payment, excessive absences, or other practices the school has deemed unacceptable.

Dean's List: Academic honor awarded for high grades earned each term.

Degree: Academic credential received by a student after finishing a program of study at a college.

Degree Audit: Evaluation from the college registrar that tracks a student's progress (courses completed, grades received) in his or her degree program.

Department: Division within a college that offers instruction in a specific subject area.

Department Chair: Faculty member who manages an academic department and addresses student concerns such as scheduling or difficulties with a faculty member.

Distance Learning: Classes or programs of study that are conducted online in a virtual, rather than actual, classroom.

E-Portfolio: Abbreviation for "electronic portfolio," a compilation of work used to provide evidence of a student's competence and achievement. Also called a digital portfolio.

Electives: Courses not specifically required for a degree. A free elective is chosen by the student. A limited or restricted elective is chosen from a specific group of courses.

Enroll: To officially select classes.

Expected Family Contribution (EFC): Amount, determined by a formula specified by law, indicating how much of a family's financial resources should be available to help pay for school.

FAFSA: Abbreviation for Free Application for Federal Student Aid, the application that everyone must complete to receive funding for college tuitions and costs.

Fee: Money charged by a college for services provided to a student. Fees are often charged for lab materials and recreational facilities.

Finals Week: Period at the end of the semester when classes do not meet and final exams are administered.

Financial Aid: Federal, state, college, and private programs that help students pay for college costs. Financial aid can be in the form of grants and scholarships, loans, or work-study programs.

Financial Aid Package: Total amount of financial aid (federal and non-federal) a student receives.

Financial Aid Counselor: College staff member who helps students and parents fill out financial aid forms and processes financial aid money.

Full-Time Faculty: Instructors (professors) of a college who are under contract for at least a complete academic year. Full-time faculty are generally involved with teaching (one to five courses), advising, and departmental and college-wide committee work.

Full-Time Student: Student who carries at least the minimum number of credits or hours to be considered "full time" by a college.

General Education Requirements: Courses in the humanities, social sciences, math, and natural sciences that provide students with a broad educational experience. Courses are typically introductory in nature and students may need to attain a satisfactory level of proficiency in areas such as Communication, Reasoning and Analysis, Information Literacy, etc.

Grade Point Average (GPA): Numeric measure of a student's overall scholastic performance in a given period or over a number of credits. Many colleges require that students maintain a minimum GPA of 2.0 to keep in good academic standing (and keep attending classes) and for eligibility for graduation.

Grant: Sum of money given to a student for the purposes of paying at least part of the cost of college. A grant does not have to be repaid.

Internship: Opportunity for students to gain practical experience in their chosen field of study.

Loan: Financial aid available to students and to the parents of students that must be repaid. In many cases, however, payments do not begin until the student finishes school.

Major: Student's primary field of study, leading to a degree in that field.

Merit-Based Financial Aid: Financial aid given to students who meet requirements not related to financial needs. Most merit-based aid is awarded on the basis of academic performance or potential and is provided as a scholarship or grants.

Mnemonics: Study method that involves organizing key concepts using each concept's first letter to create a sense or nonsense word or acronym that is easy for one to remember.

Need-Based Financial Aid: Financial aid given to students in financial need of assistance, as determined by their and their family's income and assets.

Non-Credit Course: Course in which no credit is offered toward degree requirements. However, many of these non-credit courses may count toward Financial Aid requirements.

Office Hours: Hours set aside by an instructor to meet with students.

Orientation: Program designed to assist new students in adjusting to his or her new college surroundings.

Overload: Higher number of credit hours (and courses) than is typically considered a standard load. Permission to register for an overload is often required from an academic department head or dean.

Part-Time Student: Student enrolled in a number of course credits or hours that is less than what is required for a full-time load.

Pell Grants: Federal need-based grants.

Perkins Loans: Federal financial aid program that consists of low-interest loans for undergraduates with exceptional financial need.

Plagiarism: Major form of academic dishonesty that occurs when students use the words and ideas of another without attribution, passing them off as their own.

Prerequisite: Preliminary course that must be completed before a certain course can be taken.

President: Chief administrator of the college.

Program: Set of required courses for a degree in a major area of study.

Registrar: Person in a school who manages class schedules and academic records.

Registration: Officially enrolling in classes for the upcoming grading period.

Remedial Course: Course that teaches skills needed to succeed in college-level courses. These courses are usually in the areas of math, writing, and reading.

Requirements: Set of conditions that must be met in order to do something, such as being accepted to a college, complete a degree, etc.

Resident/Non-Resident Status: Determination, for tuition purposes, of whether a student is obligated to pay resident fees or non-resident fees. Resident status typically requires having lived in the state for at least one year prior to enrollment.

Schedule of Classes: Publication (now mostly web-based) released prior to registration for the following term that includes the list of courses, faculty, sections, hours, and classroom locations.

Scholarship: Sum of money (that need not be repaid) presented to college students based on various factors such as academic achievement, community service, and extracurricular activities.

Semester: Calendar system used by schools. Schools also use trimester and quarterly calendar systems.

Stafford Loans: Student loans offered by the federal government.

Study Abroad: College coursework that students take outside the U.S., providing opportunities to experience foreign cultures and travel.

Syllabus: Overview of the assignments and activities to be included in a course.

Term: Period of time during which courses are offered.

Term Paper: Generic name for an original student paper usually due at the end of the term. Research papers are a form of term paper.

Time Management: Skill needed in college to handle all the competing demands on one's time.

Transcript: Official record of a student's educational progress. A transcript may include listings of classes, grades, major area, and degrees earned.

Transfer Credit: College credit earned at one college and applied and accepted for credit at another school.

Tuition: College fee for classroom and other instruction and the use of some facilities such as libraries.

Tutor: Experienced adult or student who helps others study a specific subject.

Waiver: When a requirement is not insisted upon, such as a prerequisite for a class or the need to pay a fee.

Withdrawal: Typically refers to the dropping of all courses for which a student is registered in a given term.

Work-Study Programs: Federal financial aid program that allows students to work part-time during the school year, usually on campus, as part of their financial aid package.

APPENDIX B:
Click Here: Useful Web Sites

Chapter 1. The Why of Community College... and the Who, What, and Where

General Information and Data About Community College

- http://www2.aacc.nche.edu
- http://www2.aacc.nche.edu/research/index.htm
  Interesting—and important—facts about community college
- http://www.petersons.com
- http://www.communitycollegereview.com
  Lists of all the community colleges in the country with links to Web sites on succeeding in community college

The Community College Experience

- http://www.ccsse.org/sense/
  Videos on "starting right" at community college
- http://www.californiareport.org/communitycolleges.jsp
  Downloadable radio pieces on succeeding at community college
- http://www.firstinthefamily.org
  Useful resources for students who are the first in their families to go to college

Accreditation

- http://www.ope.ed.gov/accreditation
  U.S. Department of Education database of accredited postsecondary schools with FAQ

Chapter 2. The Application Process in Twenty Documents or Less

General Information and Resources for Applying to Community College

- http://www.nacacnet.org/Pages/default.aspx
  Schedules of college fairs and other useful information about applying to community college
- http://www.college-admissions-secrets.com/timeline.php
  Site to help students work their way through the maze of college admissions
- http://www.knowhow2go.org/
  Video and quizzes on getting ready to apply for college

International Students

- http://www.ice.gov/sevis/index.htm
  U.S. Web site providing vital information about visa requirements, accreditation, and other important information for international students
- http://www.naces.org
  Organizations that will evaluate/translate the academic credentials of individuals who've studied outside the U.S.
- http://www.naeg.org
- http://www.edupass.org
  Information about scholarships, travel tips, and advice on making the transition to an American college

State Residency Requirements

http://www.collegegold.com/applydecide/staterequirements/
College residency requirements in your state

Students with Disabilities

- http://www.ed.gov/ocr/transition.html/
  Site with a comprehensive, downloadable pdf file on the rights of students with disabilities

Chapter 3. Money Matters

General Sites for Financial Aid

- http://www.studentaid.ed.gov
- http://www.finaid.org
  Advice and links for students seeking financial aid

FAFSA

- http://www.fafsa.ed.gov
  Essential Web site for completing and submitting FAFSA
- http://studentaid.ed.gov/PORTALSWebApp/students/english/index.jsp
  Government site helps overcome difficulties in completing the FAFSA application
- http://www.collegegoalsundayusa.org
  Lists a Sunday when you can go to locations throughout your state and get free professional help filling out the FAFSA form
- http://www.collegegold.com/applydecide/commonfafsaerrors/
  Information on common errors in filling out the FAFSA and how to avoid them
- http://www.studentaid.ed.gov/students/publications/student_guide/index.html
  How your EFC is determined in calculating your federal grant
- http://studentaid.ed.gov/students/publications/completing_fafsa/2007_2008/ques2-1.html
  National and state residency requirements for FAFSA

Financial Aid and Grant Sites

- http://www.ed.gov/programs/fpg/index.html
  Federal Pell Grants site
- http://www.fseog.com
  Site for Federal Supplemental Educational Opportunity Grant (FSEOG Program)

Scholarships

- https://www.collegedata.com/cs/search/scholar/scholar_search_tmpl.jhtml
  Includes a remarkable scholarship finder containing comprehensive lists of scholarships tailored to individual applicants
- http://www.fastweb.com
  Links to many scholarship opportunities

- https://www.coca-colascholars.org/cokeWeb/index.jsp
  The Coca-Cola Scholarship Foundation, which awards $3.4 million in two national programs
- http://americacorps.org
  Links to stipends for students involved in service projects
- http://www.hsf.net/Scholarships.aspx
  Scholarship opportunities for Latino students
- http://www.gibill.va.gov/Veterans
  Scholarship opportunities for veterans
- http://www.ptk.org/
  Scholarship opportunities for members of Phi Theta Kappa, the community college honor society

Federal Loans

- http://community.collegeanswer.com/CommunityCollege/content/index.jsp
  Sallie Mae (leading provider of student loans) Web site, which links to lots of useful information about paying for college
- http://www.staffordloan.com
  The Stafford Loan site

Employer Grants

- http://www.cael.org/lilas.htm
  Explains employer-matched, portable, employee-owned accounts used to finance education

Chapter 4. Cheers for the Adult Student

General Information for Adult Students

- http://www.back2college.com/index.shtml
  Back to college advice for adults
- http://www.agelesslearner.com/assess/
  Links to learning styles and other learning sites with tips for adult students
- http://www.nextstepmagazine.com/nextstep/ArticleList.aspx?categoryKey=12
  A collection of informative articles directed at the adult college student

Credits for Experience, Knowledge and Work

- http://www.acenet.edu/AM/Template.cfm?Section=CCRS/
  How to you determine academic credit for courses and exams taken outside traditional degree programs

- http://www.dantes.doded.mil/Dantes_web/DANTESHOME.asp
  Site reviewing procedures for getting credit for education and training in the military
- http://www.collegeboard.com/student/testing/clep/about.html
  Pass a CLEP exam and you may receive college credit

Scholarships for Adult Students
- http://www.back2college.com/library/scholarships.htm
- http://www.civicventures.org
  Sites that link to potential scholarships for returning adult students in community college

Chapter 5. ESL and Remediation: Not Just for Beginners

ESL Help and Resources
- http://www.scc-fl.edu/adulted/els/
  Site that links to a large bank of Web sites that offer advice on learning English and test-taking for ESL students
- http://a4esl.org/
- http://www.eslconnect.com/links.html
  Sites with activities, quizzes, lessons, and podcasts for people whose first language is other than English.
- http://www.learn-english-options.com
  Listening comprehension, tips on taking official English language exams, and resources for grammar
- http://www.wordchamp.com
- http://literacynet.org/cnnsf/index_cnnsf.html
  Sites where you can read current news articles with tools that teach pronunciation and grammar
- http://www.eslgold.com
- http://www.esl-lab.com
  Audio files, materials, and quizzes to test your comprehension

Chapter 6. Before You Register Read This

Choosing a Major
- http://www.scholarships.com/How-to-Choose-a-College-Major.aspx
- http://www.quintcareers.com/choosing_major.html

- http://www3.ashland.edu/services/cardev/cdm-major.html
  Sites with tips on how to choose a major and listings of federal jobs filled by college graduates with appropriate academic majors
- http://www.usajobs.gov/EI23.asp
  List of federal jobs filled by college graduates from different majors

Chapter 7. Registration and Right After—Without Losing Your Mind

Meeting with Your Advisor

- http://www.advising.vt.edu/student_resources/pma.html
- http://www.pueblocc.edu/Academics/Advising/Advisors.htm
  Advice for an effective meeting with your advisor

Textbook Sites

- http://www.prenhal.com/
- http://www.cheapesttextbooks.com
- http://campusbooks4less.com/index.html
  Sites offering comprehensive searches for textbooks available to be bought online

Chapter 8. Classified Intelligence for the Classroom

Syllabus

- http://www.ehow.com/how_2146979_read-a-syllabus.html
  Advice on how to read a syllabus effectively

Classroom Behavior

- http://www.suite101.com/article.cfm/college_success/41072
- http://www.associatedcontent.com/article/348705/costly_college_freshmen_mistakes_rude.html?cat=4
  Articles on classroom etiquette with links to specialized writing about attendance, lateness, and related classroom behavior

Dealing with Professors

- http://littleprofessor.typepad.com/the_little_professor/2007/08/notes-on-dealin.html
- http://www.ucalgary.ca/wellnessguide/professor
  General advice on interacting with professors

- http://rwuniversity.com/articles.cfm?id=18&action=show
  A professor's helpful advice on dealing with "difficult" professors
- http://www.wikihow.com/Email-a-Professor
  Rules and advice for emailing your professor with links to other professor-student issues

Office Hours

- http://talk.collegeconfidential.com/college-life/544860-what-office-hours.html
  College student Web discussion on professors' office hours

Chapter 9. Going the Distance with Distance Learning Classes

General Information on Distance Learning Classes

- http://www.onlinelearningbooks.com/learners.html
  General advice on success in online classes
- http://oregonone.org/DEquiz.htm
- http://www.ccbcmd.edu/distance/assess.html
- http://dl.austincc.edu/students/SelfAssess.html
  Sites where you can assess your suitability for a distance learning class

Glossary of Terms for Distance Learning Classes

- http://www.successdegrees.com/online-learning-courses-glossary-definitions.html
- http://www.4teachers.org/techalong/glossary
- http://www.sharpened.net/glossary/
  Dictionaries of technology and distance-learning terminology

Chapter 10. Take a Management Position in Time Management

Overcoming Procrastination

- http://www.mindtools.com/pages/article/newHTE_96.htm
- http://www.successfulacademic.com/success_tips/Overcome_procrastination.htm
- http://sas.calpoly.edu/asc/ssl/procrastination.html
  Guidelines and strategies for dealing with procrastination

Time Management Strategies

- http://www.d.umn.edu/kmc/student/loon/acad/strat/time_manage.html
- http://www.time-management-guide.com/student-time-management.html
- http://studytips.admsrv.ohio.edu/studytips/?Function=TimeMgt&Type=168hour
  Time management advice and tips targeted for students
- http://www.tadalist.com
- http://wipeelist.com
- http://voo2do.com
  Free sites with useful templates for to-do lists

Chapter 11. Please Steal These Ideas About Cheating and Plagiarism

Plagiarism

- http://gervaseprograms.georgetown.edu/honor/system/53500.html
- http://www.utoronto.ca/writing/plagsep.html
- http://www.lib.unc.edu/instruct/copyright/plagiarism/recognize.html
- http://plagiarism.umf.maine.edu/is_it.html
  Sites with tutorials and quizzes to help indentify plagiarism

Proper Footnoting and Endnotes

- http://www.loyola.edu/academics/alldepartments/history/stylesheet/foot-endnotes/
  Tutorial in using endnotes and proper footnoting
- http://www.expertvillage.com/information_546_college-higher-education.htm
  Video tutorials on formatting
- http://highered.mcgrawhill.com/sites/0078612357/student_view0/unit4/enrichment_activity_4_6.html
  Footnoting using Microsoft Word
- http://www.easybib.com
- http://citationmachine.net
- http://www.noodletools.com
- http://www.worldcat.org
  Sites that do the formatting for you
- http://www.turnitin.com
  Site that indicates how much of a submitted paper is lifted from the Web and from where

Cheating

- http://homeworktips.about.com/od/homeworktopics/a/cheating.htm
- http://www.collegebound.net/content/article/crackdown-on-college-cheating/251/

    The foolishness and dangers of cheating and overcoming the temptation

Chapter 12. The ABCs of Getting As

GPA Calculators

- http://www.foothill.edu/transfer/counseling.calc.html
- http://science.kennesaw.edu/biophys/bigGPA.html
- http://www.back2college.com/raisegpa.htm

    Sites to help you calculate your grade point average

Effective Studying

- http://ollie.dcccd.edu/Services/StudyHelp/StudySkills/#anx
- http://sas.calpoly.edu/asc/ssl.html
- http://www.how-to-study.com
- http://www.stthomas.edu/academicsupport/helpful_study_skills_links.htm
- http://www.etsu.edu/devstudy/links.htm#skills
- http://www.studygs.net
- http://www.etsu.edu/devstudy/links.htm

    Representative sites from among hundreds offering helpful information on improving study skills

Learning Styles

- http://www.metamath.com/multiple/multiple_choice_questions.html
- http://www.engr.ncsu.edu/learningstyles/ilsweb.html
- http://www.agelesslearner.com/assess/

    Self-tests to assess learning style

Research and Writing Term Papers

- http://www.library.cornell.edu/olinuris/ref/webcrit.html
- http://www.lib.berkeley.edu/TeachingLib/Guides/Internet/Evaluate.html

    Sites to help evaluate the reliability of Web sources

- http://www.dartmouth.edu/~writing/materials/student/ac_paper/what.shtml

- http://www.unc.edu/depts/wcweb/handouts/argument.html
  Helps develop skill in argumentation for papers
- http://owl.english.purdue.edu
- http://collegeuniversity.suite101.com/article.cfm/college_essay_writing_help
- http://www.utoronto.ca/writing/advise.html
  Several good sites among dozens on improving writing skills

Chapter 13. At The Test: Strategies for Your Brain and Body

Preparing for the Test

- http://www.bucks.edu/~specpop/tests.htm
- http://library.austincc.edu/help/testtake/
  Skills advice for the night before, right before, and during the test
- http://istudy.psu.edu/FirstYearModules/TestTaking/TestInformation.html
  How to overcome test anxiety

Test-Taking Strategies

- http://www.peerleader.appstate.edu/PL%20Manual/Fac_Manual/Learning_Skills/test_taking.htm
- http://www.scc-fl.edu/adulted/els/web_resources/test-taking.htm
- http://www.studygs.net/tsttak1.htm
- http://www.testtakingtips.com/test/index.htm
  Tips for the short-answer test

Essay Writing

- http://owl.english.purdue.edu/handouts/general/gl_essay.html
- http://members.tripod.com/~lklivingston/essay/links.html
- http://www.back2college.com/essaystrat.htm
  Tips for answering essay test questions

Chapter 14. So You Want to Join the Circus: Extracurricular Activities, Internships, and Study Abroad

Extracurricular Activities

- http://education.yahoo.com/college/essentials/articles/college/extracurricular_activities.htm

- http://www.helium.com/knowledge/117791-the-importance-of-extracurricular-activities-in-college
  The value of participating in extracurricular activities in college
- http://campusactivities.suite101.com/article.cfm/choosing_a_campus_activity
  How to choose an extracurricular activity

Internships

- http://internships.about.com/od/internsites/tp/internsites.htm
  Links to internship sites
- http://www.idealist.org/
  Comprehensive list of internships in the non-profit arena

Financial Resources for Study Abroad

- http://www.iie.org/programs/gilman/overview/overview.html
  Benjamin A. Gilman International Scholarship
- http://www.aifsabroad.com/scholarships.asp
  American Institute for Foreign Policy Scholarship

Chapter 15. Help Carrying Your Luggage: Transferring to a Four-Year School

General Information About the Transfer Process

- http://www.collegeanswer.com/selecting/content/sel_cc_transfer.jsp
- http://www.assist.org
- http://www.connectedu.net/corp/index.html
- http://www.collegesuccessadvice.com/transfer.html
- http://talk.collegeconfidential.com/transfer-students/497045-advice-community-college-transfer.html
- http://www.stateuniversity.com/blog/permalink/What-You-Need-to-Know-to-Be-a-Successful-Transfer-Student.html
  Discussions and advice on transferring
- http://en.wordpress.com/tag/transfer-students/

Scholarships for Transfer Students

- http://www.jkcf.org/scholarships
- http://www.collegefish.org
  General scholarship opportunities for transfers
- http://www.hsf.net/scholarships.aspx?id=452

- http://www.ptk.org/schol/schollisting.htm
- http://www.thesalliemaefund.org/smfnew/scholarship/comm_college_transfer.html
    Transfer scholarships for Latino students

Chapter 16. The Real World: Landing the First Job of Your New Career

The Résumé

- http://www.eresumes.com/
- http://monsterguide.net/how-to-write-a-resume
- http://www.soyouwanna.com/site/syws/resume/resume.html
- http://www.diversityinc.com/public/3551.cfm
- http://www.collegegrad.com/resumes
    Help for writing your résumé

The Cover Letter

- http://www.quintcareers.com/cover_letter_samples.html
- http://www.quintcareers.com/cover_letter_samples.html
- http://jobsearch.about.com/od/coverlettersamples/a/covertemplate.htm
    Advice on writing the cover letter

Interview Essentials

- http://tars.rollins.edu/careerservices/interviewingskills/index.html
- http://jobsearch.about.com/od/interviewquestionsanswers/a/interviewquest2.htm
- http://www.careercc.com/interv3.shtml
- http://www.learndirect-advice.co.uk/helpwithyourcareer/intshort/interviewquestions
- http://www.wisebread.com/how-to-answer-23-of-the-most-common-interview-questions
    Interview skills and techniques

Networking

- http://www3.lehigh.edu/alumni/career/programs/cnr/networking.asp
- http://career.berkeley.edu/Article/021011b.stm
    Advice on developing your own network

The Thank-You Note

- http://www.quintcareers.com/sample_thank-you_letters.html
- http://www.writeexpress.com/thank-you.htm
  Advice on writing the post-interview thank-you note

Chapter 17. The Last Lap: Commencement and Beyond

Preparing for Graduation

- http://www.diplomaframe.com/pages/401_22_graduation_tips_
  resources_for_college_grads.cfm
- http://campuslife.suite101.com/article.cfm/college_graduation_checklist
  Helpful hints and reminders before graduation

Graduation Day

- http://www.collegetips.com/college-graduation/tips.php
  At your graduation: overview for the big day

Notes

Chapter 1

1. The College Board, Trends in College Pricing (2008), 6, http://professionals.collegeboard.com/profdownload/trends-in-college-pricing-2008.pdf.
2. American Association of Community Colleges, "CC STATS," http://www2.aacc.nche.edu/research/index.htm.
3. Ibid.
4. Noel-Levitz, Inc., "The 2008 National Student Satisfaction and Priorities Report–Community, Junior, and Technical Colleges" (2008), 3, https://www.noellevitz.com/NR/rdonlyres/34C63D01-A37E-4929-8B83-83FBD96F59C9/0/NatSatisfactionReport2yr08.pdf.
5. Student Academic Services, Office of the President, University of California, "Community College Transfer Students at UC: Annual Report, University of California" (2000), 12, http://www.ucop.edu/sas/publish/transfer_ar2000.pdf.

Chapter 2

1. California Educational Roundtable, "Applying for Admissions," http://californiacolleges.edu/admissions/admissions.asp.
2. Envisage International Corporation, "Visa & Immigration Center," http://www.internationalstudent.com/immigration/.

Chapter 3

1. United States Government Accountability Office, "College Textbooks: Enhanced Offerings Appear to Drive Recent Price Increases" (July 2005), 8, http://www.gao.gov/new.items/d05806.pdf.
2. The College Board, "2008–09 College Prices: Keep Increases in Perspective," http://www.collegeboard.com/student/pay/add-it-up/4494.html.
3. American Association of Community Colleges, "CC STATS," http://www2.aacc.nche.edu/research/index.htm.
4. Community College Survey of Student Engagement, Essential Elements of Engagement: High Expectations, High Support (Austin: The University of Texas, Community College Leadership Program, 2008), 17, http://www.ccsse.org/publications/2008_National_Report.pdf.
5. Sam Dillon and Tamar Lewin, "Pell Grants Said to Face a Shortfall of $6 Billion," New York Times, September 17, 2008.

Chapter 4

1. Lyungai Mbilinyi, Degrees of Opportunity: Adults' Views on the Value and Feasibility of Returning to School (Minneapolis: Capella University, 2006), 2, http://www.degreesofopportunity.org/inc/degrees_opportunity_report.pdf.
2. Ibid., 7.
3. Cynthia Lak Howell, "Facilitating Responsibility for Learning in Adult Community College Students," Eric Digest (2003), 1–6.
4. Brian Pusser, et al., Return to Learning: Adults' Success in College Is Key to America's Future (Indianapolis: Lumina Foundation, 2007), 7, http://www.luminafoundation.org/publications/ReturntolearningApril2007.pdf.
5. Erin White, "Theory & Practice: Corporate Tuition Aid Appears to Keep Workers Loyal," Wall Street Journal, May 21, 2007.

Chapter 5

1. Henry Levin and Juan Carlos Calcagno, "Remediation in the Community College: An Evaluator's Perspective," Community College Review 35, no. 3 (2008): 185.
2. Jennifer Malia, "ESL College Writing in the Mainstream Classroom," Academic Exchange Quarterly, March 22, 2006, http://www.the-

freelibrary.com/ESL+college+writing+in+the+mainstream+classroom-a0146219119.

3. Alliance for Excellent Education, "Paying Double: Inadequate High Schools and Community College Remediation," Issue Brief (August 2006): 2, http://www.all4ed.org/files/archive/publications/remediation.pdf.

4. Paul Attewell, et al., "New Evidence On College Remediation," Journal of Higher Education 77, no. 5 (2006): 887.

Chapter 6

1. Susan Scrivener, et al., A Good Start: Two-Year Effects of a Freshmen Learning Community Program at Kingsborough Community College (New York: MDRC, 2008), 2, http://www.mdrc.org/publications/473/full.pdf.

2. Rob Jenkins, "The Two-Year Track: Know Thy Students," The Chronicle of Higher Education, September 27, 2005.

Chapter 7

1. Libby Sander, "At Community Colleges, A Call to Meet New Students at the Front Door," The Chronicle of Higher Education 54, no. 29 (2008): 2.

2. J. W. Elphinstone, "Strip Centers Fight to Fill Vacant Space," Atlanta Journal-Constitution, July 8, 2008, http://www.ajc.com/business/content/business/stories/2008/07/04/vacantshopsbiz.html?cxntlid=inform_sr.

3. Allen McKiel, "Survey Analysis," in 2008 Global Student E-book Survey (Palo Alto, CA: ebrary, 2008), 2, http://www.ebrary.com/corp/collateral/en/Survey/ebrary_student_survey_2008.pdf.

Chapter 8

1. Community College Survey of Student Engagement, Act on Fact: Using Data to Improve Student Success (Austin: The University of Texas, Community College Leadership Program, 2006), 12, http://www.ccsse.org/publications/CCSSESummary2006.pdf.

2. Community College Survey of Student Engagement, Engagement by Design: 2004 Findings (Austin: The University of Texas, Community Col-

lege Leadership Program, 2004), 9, http://www.ccsse.org/publications/CCSSE_reportfinal2004.pdf.

Chapter 9

1. I. Elaine Allen and Jeff Seaman, Online Nation: Five Years of Growth in Online Learning (Needham, MA: The Sloan Consortium, 2007), 5, http://www.sloan-c.org/publications/survey/pdf/online_nation.pdf.
2. Instructional Technology Council, "2007 Distance Education Survey Results: Tracking the Impact of e-Learning at Community Colleges" (2007), http://www.itcnetwork.org/file.php?file=%2F1%2FITCAnnualSurveyMarch2008.pdf.
3. Success Degrees, "Interesting Facts About Distance Learning," http://www.successdegrees.com/interesting-facts-about-distance-learning.html.
4. Instructional Technology Council, "2007 Distance Education Survey Results: Tracking the Impact of e-Learning at Community Colleges."
5. Success Degrees, "Interesting Facts About Distance Learning."
6. Online Degrees & Program Information, "All about Distance Learning," http://www.program-online-degree.com/distance_learning/distance_learning_part_one.htm.

Chapter 10

1. Steven E. Gump, "Cutting Class: Attendance as a Predictor of Student Success," College Teaching 53 (2005): 21–26.
2. Piers Steel, "The Nature of Procrastination: A Meta-Analytic and Theoretical Review of Quintessential Self-Regulatory Failure," Psychological Bulletin 133 (2007): 65–94.
3. Ibid.

Chapter 11

1. M. Lynnette Smyth and James R. Davis, "An Examination of Student Cheating in the Two-Year College," Community College Review 31 (2003) 17–32.
2. Donald McCabe and L. K. Trevino, "Cheating Among Business Students: A Challenge for Business Leaders and Educators," Journal of Management Education 19, no. 2 (1995): 205–218.

Chapter 12

1. eSchool News, "Study: Multitasking Hinders Learning," July 26, 2006, www.eschoolnews.com/news/showStory.cfm?ArticleID=6453.
2. Karin Foerde, Barbara Knowlton, and Russell Poldrack, "Modulation of Competing Memory Systems by Distraction." Proceedings of the National Academy of Sciences 103, no. 31 (2006): 11778, http://www.pnas.org/content/103/31/11778.full.pdf+html.
3. "Press Release," Association of American Publishers, August 24, 2005, http://www.publishers.org/main/PressCenter/Archicves/2005_Aug/Aug_07.htm.
4. University of Illinois, "Studying for Exams," http://www.uic.edu/depts/ace/study_exams.shtml.
5. Yoo Seung-Schik, et al., "A Deficit in the Ability to Form New Human Memories Without Sleep," Nature Neuroscience 10 (2007): 385.
6. Christie Nicholson, "Rest Assured: The Brain Practices the Day's Lessons as We Sleep," Scientific American, August 5, 2008.
7. The Center for Public Education, "Research Review: What Research Says About the Value of Homework" (February 2007), http://www.centerforpubliceducation.org/site/c.kjJXJ5MPIwE/b.2479409/k.BF59/Research_review_What_research_says_about_the_value_of_homework.htm.

Chapter 13

1. R. Lee and M. Balick, "Rx: Caffeine," EXPLORE: The Journal of Science and Healing 2, no. 1 (2006): 55.
2. Mayo Clinic Staff, "Stress Relief from Laughter? Yes, No Joke," July 23, 2008, http://www.mayoclinic.com/health/stress-relief/SR00034.

Chapter 15

1. Community College Survey of Student Engagement, Engagement by Design: 2004 Findings (Austin: The University of Texas, Community College Leadership Program, 2004), 4, http://www.ccsse.org/publications/CCSSE_reportfinal2004.pdf.
2. Roger Schultz, "Transferring: More Benefits Than You Might Realize," The International Education Site, http://www.intstudy.com/study_abroad/livfiles/saww6a14.htm.

Chapter 16

1. EssayInfo.com, "Resume Writing: The Importance of Your Resume," http://essayinfo.com/resume/resume_importance.php.
2. Gerry Crispin and Mark Mehler, "CareerXroads 7th Annual Source of Hire Study: What 2007 Results Mean for Your 2008 Plans" (2008), http://www.careerxroads.com/news/SourcesOfHire08.pdf.
3. Patrik Karlsson, "Please Send a Thank You Note After the Job Interview" (June 2008), http://www.amazines.com/Career/article_detail.cfm/510096?articleid=510096.
4. WriteExpress, "Thank-You Letters," http://www.writeexpress.com/thank-you.htm.

Chapter 17

1. Northwest State Community College, "Graduation Information," http://www.northweststate.edu/Current_Students/Registrars_Office/Graduation_Information.html.
2. Family Care Foundation, "If the World Were a Village of 100 People," from State of the Village Report, Donella H. Meadows (2005), http://www.familycare.org/news/if_the_world.htm.

About the Authors

DR. DEBRA GONSHER is the Chairperson of the Communication Arts & Sciences Department and former coordinator of the Humanities Division at Bronx Community College of the City University of New York. A three-time Emmy award–winning documentary filmmaker, she is the author of the college textbook *CareerSpeak: Articulation and Presentation.*

DR. JOSHUA HALBERSTAM is an Associate Professor in the Department of Communication Arts & Sciences at Bronx Community College, and has taught at New York University and Teachers College, Columbia University. He is the author of eight books, including *Everyday Ethics* and *Acing College* and has recently published his first novel, *A Seat at the Table.*